CLICK TO CALM

Healing the Aggressive Dog

CLICK TO CALM

Healing the Aggressive Dog

by Emma Parsons, APDT, NADOI

Karen Pryor
Clickertraining

Published by Sunshine Books, Inc.
49 River Street, Suite 3
Waltham, MA 02453
781-398-0754
www.clickertraining.com

ISBN-13: 978-1-890948-20-7
ISBN 1-890948-20-9
Printed in Canada

Library of Congress Number: 2004117147

9 8 7 6 5 4 3

This book is available at quantity discounts for multiple-copy purchases.

Contents

Preface

This book is about healing the aggressive dog through meticulous management and clicker training. Please note that I deliberately do not define the word aggression anywhere in this book. Though one can scientifically research aggression in all its various forms, and I suggest that you do, the term "aggression" in this book indicates any behavior that frightens you or makes you feel uncomfortable when it is displayed. It may be a dog that has snapped or growled once or it can be a dog that has repeatedly bitten another dog or a human.

Before I treat my clients' dogs, I take a very detailed history of the dog's behavior, including what other training techniques were used on the dog. I classify every behavior as either desirable or undesirable. Aggression is, after all, a normal canine behavior; you may or may not, depending on the situation, want your dog to display the behavior. A dog that displays aggression inappropriately, no matter the cause, can be dangerous to live with, especially for families with children.

I take into account how my client perceives his or her dog's behavior. One client may wish to end the life of a dog that has growled once, while another client, who is bitten on a regular basis, finds this behavior acceptable.

Whatever the client's level of anxiety, I focus on the undesirable behavior and the circumstances that can cause it to happen. I then teach my client how to lessen the intensity of the given behavior, and if possible, to eradicate the behavior entirely.

Before treating any dog, I recommend that the dog have a full physical exam as well as a complete set of blood work, a thyroid profile, and a urinalysis. We need to know whether or not the aggression is caused by an underlying medical condition and take care of those problems first. Hormonal diseases, organ dysfunction (kidney and liver disease), diseases affecting the nervous system (e.g., epilepsy, brain tumors) and urinary tract, declining eyesight or hearing, and any illness or condition that may cause pain or discomfort are all possible causes of aggressive behavior.

If the dog appears to be in good health, the next step, in the most serious of cases, is to have a veterinary behaviorist evaluate the dog to see if anti-anxiety drugs or other pharmaceuticals are appropriate. Getting the dog on the right medication before beginning a clicker training program is a good idea. When implemented correctly, both treatments work together, and can change a dog's life—and the owner's—permanently.

Emma Parsons

Acknowledgments

I never thought I would be one to write a book. If someone had told me twenty years ago that I would one day be teaching dog owners how to help heal their aggressive pets through clicker training, I would have thought that they were terribly mistaken!

For some people, writing a book is a life's dream. For me, after studying with Karen Pryor, it was a necessity.

Karen Pryor, you are my hero! Thank you for introducing me to the methodology of clicker training and teaching me how to shape aggression, like any other behavior, in accordance with the laws of learning. You had more faith in me than I had in myself as I struggled through my dog Ben's toughest years. And thank you for allowing me to call you numerous times, late at night, to gleefully tell you that, "My gosh, the clicker really worked again with this aggressive dog!" Who knew?

Karen, you are my role model and my mentor. I am so blessed for having known you; thank you for not only being my precious teacher, but also for personally accepting me into your family.

Thanks to Joan Bolker, for teaching me how to fearlessly put my thoughts down on a blank piece of paper, and to Gale Pryor, my editor, without whose unlimited patience and understanding this book simply would not exist.

Linda Holway, you were my first teacher and are one of my closest friends. Thank you for introducing me to the world of dogs, a world I could not live without.

Patty Ruzzo, it was you who taught me the meaning of perfection and how it can be attained by "practicing perfect!" Thank you, also, for allowing Ben to play with your own competition dogs, regardless of how ill-behaved he could be. I will always treasure our friendship.

Kris Pemberton, you were one of the only friends who actually saw Ben at his worst. Thank you for encouraging me to learn more and to not lose hope. Big hugs go to the staff at VCA Rotherwood Animal Hospital in Newton, Mass. You are my family who have known Ben since he was a baby. Thank you for protecting him from other dogs and accommodating him whenever it was medically necessary.

Dr. Devin Scruton, you are such a gifted and talented veterinarian! Thank you for keeping Ben, as well as all my other dogs, happy and healthy. I especially appreciate your willingness to always be open-minded to some of my "strange" ideas, and for allowing me to call you anytime, day or night, with questions or concerns.

Special thanks to the following trainers/communicators who gave me the gift of their friendship and helped me to put the pieces of the puzzle together: Jennifer Kessner, Leslie Nelson, Robert Bailey and the late Marian Breland Bailey, Diane Smart, Susan Latham, Marcia Zais, and Mary Anne Callahan.

Dr. Patricia McConnell, Jean Donaldson, Turid Rugaas, and James O'Heare, you were my inspiration from a distance.

Ben would not have been able to practice interacting with stable, nonreactive dogs if it hadn't been for all of you who allowed him to do so with your dogs: Israel Meir, Geoff Stern and RoseAnne Mandell, Anya Wittenborg, Jean Berman, Rick Wood, Ellen Brinker, Margaret Stubbs, Barbara Beckedorff, Susan Conant, Roo Grubis, Louis Massa, Cathy Shea, Virginia Parsons, Joel Wolff, and Penny Schultz.

I wish to thank my family members, especially my husband, Gregory, who had to put up with my absences and my required solitude while I was working on "the book." Thanks also to my mom, Irene Spinelli, who is my constant source of strength.

Benjamin, my beloved golden retriever, you are my soul mate. I've learned more from you than from any human being on earth. You have taught me how to love unconditionally and to be strong no matter what the situation. You have taught me what it means to put my life in God's hands and to be a servant to my fellow human beings as well as their dogs. I am a changed person because of your most intimate gifts.

Nicholas, my rescued keeshond, who came into my life without so much as a collar on your neck, you are my shadow, my constant companion. You, too, have been an inspiration. Thank you for wanting to work with me and for becoming a beautiful working dog, so that I could still continue to show in obedience and freestyle while I was rehabilitating Ben. You, my friend, far surpassed all of the goals I had even for Ben. You allowed me to experience the best of both worlds!

Last (but by no means least), I must thank my students, who continue to amaze and inspire me by their constant creativity in solving some of the most difficult canine aggression issues via the clicker.

Emma Parsons, *December 2004*

Introduction

This book is written to share with you what I have learned in treating Ben, my golden retriever. Ben used to attack other dogs. Now he no longer does, thanks to patient handling and clicker training.

Ben was, and remains, my instrument and my teacher. He has been the catalyst for everything I do and teach as a dog trainer. I count among my friends some of the most talented trainers and behaviorists in the country—all of whom I have met through Ben.

The gifts that I have received from Ben not only improved my dog training skills but also brought me face-to-face with the person that I was and the person I have become. Once I didn't mind what punishment Ben would have to endure in our attempts to rid him of his aggression problem. As long as the behavior was going to be fixed, how we got there didn't matter. If a trainer had told me that he was going to hang Ben by his toes from the ceiling for two hours, I would have said, "Fine! As long as it stops the aggression."

My work with Ben at that time was all about me: my goals, my aspirations, what I wanted to accomplish in the obedience ring. I eventually learned, however, that my goals had nothing to do with my dog. I trained the way I thought I had to in order to get the reliable behavior that I so eagerly sought. The dog had no choice in the matter.

The process of treating Ben's aggression through positive reinforcement, however, has taught me the importance of putting the needs of my dog before my own needs and wants. Whether it's one of my own dogs or a client's dog, the needs of that particular dog come first. As a traditional trainer, this was a difficult lesson for me. Owning an aggressive dog can be a devastating experience, not to mention a litigious one. The experience can make you feel hopeless; in fact, for the thousands of dogs put down each year because of their aggressive behavior, it is hopeless. As a result of my work with Ben, and subsequently with many other aggressive dogs, I now believe that almost every case of aggression can be helped through positive training and careful management. Aggression can never be erased completely, but it can be calmed.

I purchased Ben as a puppy, intending to take him to the highest level of obedience I could. I wanted to train him correctly right from the start, to begin with a fresh, clean slate, doing the right thing every step of the way. As an obedience instructor, I have successfully helped many clients raise their unseasoned puppies to become confident dogs. Many have gone on to become accomplished obedience and agility competitors, pet therapy dogs, and more. I certainly knew how to raise a puppy properly. Or so I thought.

Ben was socialized early to people and other dogs. I exposed him to environments in which loud noises and commotion prevailed. I began formal obedience training with him at the age of five months, using purely positive training techniques. Patty Ruzzo, a superb obedience competitor, was our teacher. Ben loved his work. He loved to heel, jump, and retrieve whatever objects we presented to him that day. All was well in our world until Ben was about seven months old. An incident that occurred around that time foretold the problems to come.

Ben and I had just finished a lesson at a friend's training center when a woman came in with her Welsh corgi. As we walked down the narrow corridor to leave the building, the corgi snarled at Ben, and Ben retorted with a low growl. I looked down in amazement at my exuberant boy. He seemed quite proud of himself. While his behavior surprised me, I didn't think much about it.

As the months went by, however, the intensity of Ben's aggressive displays began to increase. He lunged, barked, and growled at other dogs for no apparent reason. In the beginning, Ben's aggression was directed only toward some dogs. There didn't seem to be a common thread among the dogs that would cause Ben to react. Dogs of different sizes, colors, and genders could all set him off. His growl evolved into a full-blown tirade. My apprehension grew. None of my other dogs had ever so much as lifted a lip at another dog, even if the other dog was clearly threatening them.

Aggressive? My dog aggressive? Not on your life. I was in complete denial. Ben was just reacting strongly to other dogs, I told myself. He couldn't be aggressive. Aggressive dogs are trained to be that way, or traumatized at some point. They guard junkyards and drug dealer's homes—not my yard, not my home. No matter what I told myself, however, Ben's bad behavior increased and intensified.

Another incident, which happened one night when I was taking Ben to his obedience class, made me realize I had to do something about this disturbing behavior. As Ben and I were walking to class, I saw a friend with her malamute and we stopped to say hello. Ben took one look at my friend's dog and had a fit. He lunged at the end of his leash, growling in the malamute's face. That was it! I'd had it! I could not tolerate Ben going after my friends' dogs. I wanted this behavior more than under control—I wanted it totally gone.

Accepting at last that I needed help, I spoke with Ben's breeder and we agreed Ben should be neutered. We hoped the procedure might improve his behavior. It did not.

I decided to consult an expert. Most obedience teachers are not comfortable working with aggressive behavior. I couldn't blame them; I never wanted to deal with it either. A friend, however, suggested that I call an aggression expert she knew who had a great reputation. I quickly made an appointment.

As planned, I met the expert at a local park. I packed my bag that morning with a martingale collar, some tug toys, and lots of food treats that I knew Benny adored. My husband, Greg, dropped off Ben and me and went to find a parking space. As we were walking across the parking lot to class, I recognized the trainer from a distance and waved to him. As he walked toward us, with his German shepherd at his side, Ben growled and lunged at the shepherd.

Suddenly the trainer put his dog in the down position and proceeded to show me how we would deal with Ben's aggression in the future. He took Ben's leash out of my hands and jerked Ben off the ground, hanging him by his prong collar. Ben bared all his teeth at this strange person and quite sensibly tried to get away. While I had seen Ben growl at other dogs, I had never seen him bare his teeth at a person. Ben's fearful response was met with an even harder correction, which did not stop until Ben surrendered. Moments after the ordeal ended, Ben defecated all over himself.

My hands were shaking as I tried to gather up my leash to follow the trainer to class. Greg, who had just finished parking the car, couldn't believe his eyes. He was angry that I had allowed this man to hurt our dog. I tried to explain that punishment is commonly used in dealing with aggression. The idea was that, having been so severely punished, Ben would never dare growl at another dog again. But even I had not expected such a horrific incident.

During the class, Ben was sullen. He allowed the teacher to heel him around numerous dogs repeatedly and never made a sound. Handing the leash back to me at the end of the class, the teacher told me that Ben was cured and that in the future, should he ever be aggressive toward another dog, I was to hang him on the prong collar just as he had done.

I was skeptical. Not only did I doubt that I could ever treat Ben in such a harsh manner, but I had a feeling that this was not the last I would see of his problem behavior.

A week later I decided to take Ben to an area obedience class to see if the corrections that were administered by the aggression expert were still effective. I loaded him in the car with all his training paraphernalia and off we went. After taking all the training equipment into the building, I went back outside to bring in Ben. I attached his leash to his collar and led him out of my car.

On seeing another dog, Ben instantly flew into a rage. Growling, screaming, and teeth bared, he lunged violently at the end of his leash. Foam dripped out of both sides of his mouth as the explosion raged on. There was no end to this; seconds turned into minutes as I dragged him painfully back into my car. Once there he started to vomit. He only calmed down after I began driving away.

I was flabbergasted and shaken. What would I do now? Ben's behavior had actually gotten worse since the session with the aggression expert. How was I supposed to deal with so violent a reaction? I felt certain that in Ben's mind the mere presence of another dog meant possible death.

I understand now that it was the timing of the trainer's punishment of Ben that was incorrect and disastrous. If there had ever been a moment when the punishment could have been executed effectively, it would have been before the trainer paused to put his shepherd in the down position. Because time had elapsed, Ben associated the severe punishment with the presence of the other dog rather than with his own behavior. The trainer actually corrected Ben just when he had begun to quiet down following his initial aggressive response.

Convinced that even dogs in a down position were a deadly threat, Ben's comfort zone in the presence of other dogs had shrunk to nonexistent. No matter how far away or submissive another dog was, he would explode. Ben even began to act aggressively when a car door would open; I think he expected a dog to jump out. Jingling car keys would set him off; the noise must have sounded like the jingling of another dog's collar tags.

This book is the culmination of the journey that I have taken with Ben since that day in the park. Through the years, I have met with various trainers all over the country, and have attended many seminars aimed at helping handlers and trainers understand and treat aggression. No one trainer had all the right answers, nor do I profess to have them all. Instead I found that each teacher I consulted contributed a tiny piece toward solving the puzzle of how to manage Ben's aggressive behavior.

The biggest piece of the puzzle was contributed by my friend and mentor, Karen Pryor, who introduced me to clicker training. Karen helped me learn to read Ben's canine signals accurately, unhindered by my own emotion. She taught me to click and treat him simply for being in the presence of other dogs, and showed me how to develop several behaviors incompatible with aggression that Ben could perform while in these situations. She was the one, who during one of Ben's fits in class, came over, gently put her hand on my arm and calmly said, "Emma, it is only behavior."

"Only behavior?" I gasped. Could it be so simple? This "behavior" had caused me so much grief in my life, both personally and professionally. It had become a source of tension in my marriage and almost caused me to lose several friendships. If I walked Ben on the street or in the park, strangers asked why I was abusing my dog by walking him around on that "muzzle." I had learned to lie and told them that Ben had been abused. (He had been in a way.) I didn't care; at least this response would invoke some kind of understanding, some kind of sympathy. I was desperate for support and encouragement from anyone! I had allowed Ben's aggression to balloon into a problem that took over our lives. I found hope that night in class, with Karen's calm words: "It's only behavior." After all, through positive reinforcement, behavior—any behavior—can be changed.

The Road to Recovery

Ben will never be a completely calm, secure dog. He remains fearful and wary of new situations and new environments. The disastrous punishment he received magnified an already sensitive temperament. It required a year of careful handling just to be able to bring Ben into an obedience class without him exploding at every dog he saw. It took another year for him to perform simple, known behaviors such as sits, downs, and recalls in a group class. His heeling behavior was the most difficult to attain. At one point, I thought it would be impossible. But we took it step by step, session by session. Now Ben is able to heel in a class situation, happily and willingly, the entire time. At one time I had been repeatedly advised to put Ben to sleep; now he is alive, calm, and able to accompany me wherever I go.

Since my work began with Ben, I have helped many clients with aggressive dogs use the same patient, positive methods. Some clients have been experienced trainers, others inexperienced pet owners. All have been able to learn and employ these clicker training techniques to help their dogs develop new behaviors incompatible with aggression.

How did clicker training calm Ben and my clients' aggressive dogs? With a clicker and the principles of operant conditioning, you can shape the emotional state of an animal just as you can shape any other behavior. Simply clicking and treating dogs calms them. As the dog performs the behavior you asked for, he is not thinking about his fear or anything else that may make him uncomfortable. A busy dog has no time to be fearful. His focus is on the task at hand. The dog, therefore, is able to make decisions, even in a threatening environment. The day Ben saw another dog coming toward him and, instead of flying into a tirade, looked up at me for a click and a treat, was the day I knew that we would succeed.

Many of the techniques you will find in this book were developed in response to my own fear of handling Ben in public places. No matter how hard I tried while out walking I could not relax the tension on my leash. If I saw another dog coming toward us, I sucked in my breath and, unconsciously, pulled up on the leash.

One day I did an experiment. I took Ben out into my yard. It was just us with no other dogs around. I leash walked him as I normally would. As I walked, I suddenly sucked in my breath and tightened up on my leash. Ben became just as forcefully aggressive as he did when he would see another dog out in public. Only this time his head was moving back and forth, scanning the perimeters of the yard; he was convinced that there was another dog in the immediate area. My behavior and tight leash had become his cue to aggressive behavior.

Instead of trying to control my response (tightening the leash), which I felt might be impossible if we actually were faced with another dog, I changed Ben's response to the "tight leash" cue. Through clicker training I was able to teach Ben that the tight leash meant to establish eye contact with me quickly. Once I had the eye contact, I could ask him to perform a behavior incompatible with aggression.

Eventually I was able to teach Ben how to greet other dogs appropriately on cue as well as how and when to use his "calming signals," the canine aggression cutoff signals. As Turid Rugaas states in her book *On Talking Terms with Dogs: Calming Signals*, "The signals are used at an early state to prevent things from happening, avoiding threats from people and dogs, calming down nervousness, fear, noise, and unpleasant things. Examples of calming signals are: licking the lips, turning the head, play bowing, etc." Through clicker training, I could put all these social behaviors on cue.

Ben is now seven years old and is a different dog. At the age of four, he received his United Kennel Club Companion Dog Title in a single weekend, placing in the ribbons for all three shows. At five, he passed the American Kennel Club's Canine Good Citizen test. This test required that Ben meet a strange dog appropriately on leash. He passed with flying colors.

Ben's Statistics

After two months:	Ben began to eat after being clicked.
After six months:	Ben could enter an environment in which other dogs were present without an aggressive display. He could not, however, also perform known obedience behaviors.
After one year:	Ben could reliably perform single-cued behaviors in the presence of other dogs. Heeling was the last behavior to be perfected in this environment.

CHAPTER 1

Clicker Home Management

There is no magic to the technology we call clicker training, other than that it offers a universal language that can be "spoken" by all species. The clicker provides a simple, clear form of communication between verbal humans and nonverbal animals. The sound of the clicker means the same thing, every time, to every participant.

Information is empowering to any animal and helps to shape its attitude toward the environment in which it lives. Once the animal realizes that it is in control of its own environment and the consequences of its actions, its confidence grows. The sound of the click represents the successful attainment of information that the animal needs to succeed. With this success comes joy and confidence for both trainer and trainee.

This confidence-building is why clicker training has dramatic results with animals in shelters, for example. Dogs and cats that have been abandoned have no sense of self. Everything they know and love has been taken away. Nothing in their environment smells or sounds familiar. The clicker, however, gives them a reliable method of understanding and communicating in a totally alien environment. It provides security in the midst of insecurity. Clicker-trained shelter animals show a quiet confidence in sharp contrast to their kennel mates' frantic barking. No wonder they are adopted more quickly and more likely to be kept.

Clicker training puts the focus on what the animal is doing right instead of what the animal is doing wrong. The clicker trainer looks for and captures positive pieces of behavior instead of negative. It is in this framework that the relationship between human and animal is shaped and defined. The relationship is built on trust and the trainer's respect for the animal's decision-making capabilities. This relationship is not based on one dominating the other; it is a partnership between human and animal that is fluent and alive.

The beauty of the clicker is that it is a convenient, quick, clear, and precise marker signal. It is void of emotion and its meaning is not open to interpretation. It signifies clarity and confidence to the animal even when the trainer might be hesitant or fearful, as is often the case with owners who are trying to work with their aggressive dogs. The clicker gives you the ability to communicate directly with your dog, regardless of the setting or circumstances. You can mark or capture behavior that will be gone in an instant. Only the clicker gives you the ability to pinpoint a millisecond of calm behavior in a stream of aggressive behavior.

The clicker's clarity soon comes to signify confidence to a dog, regardless of whether the handler feels confident or not. You can "hide" your insecurities behind the clicker. Your hand may be shaking as you click, but your dog, who is focused on the click, will never suspect your weakened state. Clicker training your dog tells him that you are totally in control of the situation, even when you don't feel in control at all. It is very important, when exposing your dog to an environment in which he feels insecure, that under your guidance he feels safe, and that you see nothing dangerous in the situation.

How to Clicker Train

Clicker training is a positive-reinforcement training system, based on the principles of operant conditioning, that incorporates the use of a marker signal (the click) to tell the animal precisely what it was doing right at that point in time. Behaviors that are marked by the click, and therefore reinforced, are more likely to happen again. Dogs learn very quickly that click equals treat. The trainer "clicks" (marks the desired behavior) and then gives the animal a piece of favorite food or another reward for which the dog will work.

The strength of this method comes from the pairing of an event marker with a reward. The sound of the click becomes associated with a positive reward, thereby becoming rewarding in and of itself. It is therefore called a "conditioned reinforcer" or "secondary reinforcer." The reward is the primary reinforcer. A primary reinforcer does not need an association or explanation that it is good.

The premise of clicker training is quite simple: you see the behavior, you mark it with a click, and you reward the behavior. It is crucial that the click be followed immediately by a primary reinforcer. Food treats work well here, especially if you are "on location." When you first start working with your dog, make sure to maintain an extremely high rate of reinforcement. In other words, click and feed the heck out of your dog!

You should use clicker training for new behavior only. As your dog becomes more skilled at the learned behavior, you can switch your signal from the click to a verbal marker like "Yes!" or "Good!" You will then reward your dog on a variable rate of reinforcement, which means that you will reinforce every correct response unpredictably.

If you have never worked with the clicker, there are some wonderful books to help get you started (see Resources, page 179). You can use clicker training to teach your dog obedience behaviors, tricks, sport behaviors, and yes, even to control his aggression. If you've never tried clicker training before, read one of the suggested books or attend a seminar or clicker class. Learn the techniques and understand the concept so that you are comfortable with it.

Clicker Training to Treat Aggression

One of the major benefits of clicker training to treat aggression is that it incorporates both classical and operant conditioning principles simultaneously to help us desensitize and "reprogram" our dogs. By clicking and feeding the dog in an aversive environment, you not only change the dog's emotional association with that environment (classical conditioning) but you can also pinpoint every correct decision the dog makes while he "operates" in the environment (operant conditioning).

Another benefit is that the click always means the same thing, every time. When the animal hears the click, it knows that whatever it was doing at that precise moment in time was the reason it got rewarded. And when you are trying to capture the absence of aggressive behavior (e.g., the animal taking a breath in between snarling and growling), no tool other than a clicker—certainly not your voice—can mark these momentary behaviors as precisely. Bob Bailey once expressed the exactness of the clicker in saying, "It is the 'scalpel' in teaching intricate behaviors."

Behavior taught via the clicker has the tendency to become indelibly engraved in the mind of the animal that you are teaching. It is not forgotten. Science has not yet explained why this is true, yet experienced clicker trainers have their theories. Clicker-trained behavior quickly becomes an animal's "default behavior." When an animal is in an uncertain state of mind, it displays a clicker-trained behavior more frequently than behaviors it learned through aversive or punishment-based training.

Simply hearing a click physiologically calms your dog. Karen Pryor explains one possible reason why: "The power of the clicker may well be in the possible relationship between clicking and the amygdala, a structure in the limbic system, or oldest part of the brain. Research in neurophysiology has identified the kinds of stimuli—bright lights, sudden sharp sounds—that reach the amygdala first, before reaching the cortex, or thinking part of the brain. The click is that kind of stimulus."

Other research on conditioned fear responses in humans shows that these also are established via the amygdala and are characterized by a pattern of very rapid learning (often on a single trial), long-term retention, and a big surge of concomitant emotions.

We clicker trainers see similar patterns of very rapid learning, long retention, and emotional surges, albeit with positive emotions rather than fear responses. It may be that the clicker is a conditioned "joy" stimulus that is acquired and recognized by the same primitive pathways, which would help explain why it is so different from, say, a human word in its effect.

Is it possible that the sound of the click is not only physiologically calming for your dog, but also for you? As the handler of a dog with aggressive responses, you feel a great deal of tension yourself. If the process of clicking your dog reduces that tension, then you are clicking and calming yourself as well. You are providing yourself with the default behavior of observing, clicking, and reinforcing your dog, rather than exhibiting your own tension and fear. This is the gift of clicker training for those handlers, like me, whose hands shake as we expose our dogs to situations we both find aversive.

Stranger in a Strange Land: Communicating with Your Dog

Dogs rely on the structure that we provide for them; they need this structure to live in our human world appropriately and successfully. Unless taught, they have no way to communicate with us. When they are given no instructions, no boundaries, they experiment with their behavior to find out what consequences will follow. They are simply seeking information. Humans are the same way; when we enter a foreign environment, are surrounded by strangers and unable to communicate, we too seek information and understanding.

Imagine you arrive for the first day of a new job as a secretary in an office. You shyly tell the receptionist who you are and she guides you to the appropriate department. Once there, you see that other people are working diligently behind their desks. No one, however, looks up as you enter the room. You continue looking around the room, hoping to make some sort of visual contact. Finally someone looks up (your boss, perhaps?) and points you toward a desk. You go there and sit. The desk is empty. You are not sure what you should do next. "Where is the bathroom?" you wonder as your confusion turns to tension.

Compare that scenario to this one: Your first day on the job, you shyly tell the receptionist who you are and she accompanies you to the appropriate department. Once there, she introduces you to Sally, the person in charge (you breathe a sigh of relief). Sally introduces you to the other employees whom you will be working with and shows you to your desk. After you put your things down, she shows you where the cafeteria and the bathrooms are. Once back at your desk, she gives you a short letter to type. "I will come back to get you at noon so that I can introduce you to several more employees at lunch," Sally says as she leaves your office.

Which company would you rather work for? Both are foreign environments to you as you enter the building on the first day of your new job. In what situation would you feel most comfortable? Wouldn't you choose the company that provides the structure and the information that you need in order to feel successful?

Unfortunately, dogs most often endure the first scenario. They enter a new family's house, they don't speak the language, and they have no idea what they're supposed to do. Dogs are not born knowing how to live in a human household. They need to be shown appropriate behavior in a way that they can understand. They need structure and information in order to be successful.

The most important lesson we need to teach all our dogs, whether or not they exhibit aggressive behavior, is that they have to learn to respect all the human members of the family. Teaching this is a two-pronged process. First, we need to establish structure for our dogs in our living environment; we can use "clicker home management" for this. Second, we need to establish a common vocabulary with our dogs; for this, clicker training delivers the information they need.

Leadership Without Confrontation: Ten Principles of Clicker Home Management

In any healthy relationship between a handler and a dog, the human needs to be the one to make all the important decisions in her dog's life. Most dogs will naturally assume the leadership role if there is no obvious hierarchy present. If the human allows this to happen, the dog feels that he is the one in charge and, subsequently, that he has to discipline other members of the family. Dogs are likely to discipline in the most direct way they know how: with their teeth!

The following clicker home management program will help you teach your dog that you are the leader; you can do this without frightening or threatening him. The program establishes a balanced handler/dog relationship, and teaches your dog to trust and respect you without requiring that you prove your dominance over the dog. Most dogs are less stressed when they leave the decision-making responsibilities to their handlers. As you begin to expose your dog to stressful environments, your dog needs to rely on you for his safety. Your dog must learn to trust your judgment, allowing you to make decisions for him.

Implement one or two of the following ten principles of clicker home management every week or so, depending on how fast your dog progresses. When you introduce a new training program, a dog's behavior sometimes worsens before it gets better. Be patient and persistent through the bumps as you reshape the dynamics of your relationship with your dog.

Principle #1: Teach your dog to "say please"

If your dog wants you to do something for him—pat him or play with him, for example—first ask him to perform some kind of familiar behavior for you as a way of "saying please." It is only polite! A sit works well here. Click the dog as he sits and then give the dog what it was that he wanted, whether a pat or a game. If your dog ignores your request, turn and walk away. Do not look at the dog. Do not stand in front of the dog repeating "Sit. Sit. Sit!" Do not engage the dog in any way, even with your eyes, for approximately 30 seconds. Go into a different room if you must, closing the door behind you. After a pause, call the dog to you and ask for the behavior again.

Let's say your dog wants to sit with you while you are watching TV. Without asking first with a polite sit, he jumps uninvited onto the sofa and plops down next to you. You stand up and motion for him to get off. He does not relinquish his space voluntarily so you gently escort him off. You can accomplish this either by taking him by his collar and gently guiding him down or, if your dog is collar sensitive, by attaching a six-foot nylon line (available at most hardware stores) to your dog's collar and guiding him using the end of the line. Ignore him for a couple of minutes, avoiding eye contact. After a couple of minutes have passed, call him to you and ask him to sit. (Remember to give the cue only once.) Click as he folds into a sit. Behavior completed! If you ask him to sit and he doesn't, lure him into the sit position with a treat. Click as he folds into the sit and feed him his treat. Once the behavior is completed, invite him up onto the sofa to sit beside you. If at any time you have to get up from the couch, call him to go with you. Click and give him a treat for accompanying you into the kitchen. Ask him for another sit before letting him back up on the couch to sit beside you.

Principle #2: Catch your dog being good

Dogs crave attention. They absolutely love positive interaction, but if the humans in the household are too busy to interact with the dog on a regular, day-to-day basis, they'll seek negative attention just as eagerly as they seek positive attention.

Unfortunately, we tend to notice our dogs more frequently when they exhibit what we consider inappropriate canine behavior. Aggressive behavior catches one's attention especially quickly. In households with more than one dog, the dog that only gets attention when he attacks the other dog in the house can quickly become a dangerous nuisance.

Let's take the case of Colby, a newly adopted two-year-old golden retriever. A family of four with two children, ages ten and fourteen, recently brought him home. Colby enters into his new home and sniffs in every room. The children follow as he roams the house. In the hours that follow, Colby picks up a new baseball glove and parades around the house with it hanging from his mouth. One of the kids, upset that Colby might damage his new purchase, scolds Colby and chases him. Finally he tackles Colby and tries to pull the glove out of the dog's mouth. Colby growls. The boy backs away as Colby begins to chew the glove.

The next evening the family gathers in the living room to watch a movie. Colby goes over to his basket of new toys and takes out one of his stuffed animals. He happily prances around the room with his purple dinosaur. He looks up at the family members but no one seems to notice. Puzzled by the lack of attention, Colby drops his toy and goes running into the kitchen. Winter boots are drying by the back door. He picks up one of the boots and throws it in the air. Dad hears the thud as the boot hits the floor and comes to see what Colby is up to. Colby picks up the boot, and Dad gives chase. Mom joins in. As she reaches down to take the boot out of his mouth, Colby growls. She backs away. What is Colby learning? What behavior gives the dog the attention that he wants? What behavior causes the humans to respond in a way that fulfills Colby's desires? Where will this behavior pattern lead for Colby?

As humans we like to "talk to" behavior by scolding our dogs. Whenever a behavior receives a response, even if the response is a scolding, the behavior is reinforced. Any behavior that is looked at and talked to—nicely or not—will be maintained to some degree. Behavior that is ignored will eventually disappear. Colby is quickly learning that chewing on some objects gains him the attention that he craves and that growling allows him to continue that chewing. When Colby behaves appropriately by human standards, he is ignored; but when he creates a commotion of some kind, whether by chewing a shoe or taking a child's toy, he has total control over his environment.

If Colby's family focused instead on catching him being good and always reinforcing the good behavior, the story would have quite a different conclusion. Institute Principle #2 of clicker home management by praising your dog when he is chewing one of his own toys instead of your shoe. Pat your dog when he is sitting quietly by your side instead of jumping in your lap. Click and feed your dog when he periodically checks in with you while out walking in the woods instead of running away and not coming back when he's called. Behavior that is reinforced will continually be repeated. Reinforce only the behaviors that you want to see again!

Principle #3: Calm gets you everything, noisy gets you nothing

Attention-seeking behaviors such as barking and whining are as unacceptable as outright misbehaviors. If your dog demands your attention in any way other than behaving desirably, ignore him. Get up and leave the room if you must. Shut the door behind you. Pay attention to the dog only after he has abandoned whatever pushy, annoying behavior he has displayed. This also holds true for the overexcited dog that greets his owner at the end of a workday by pummeling him or her at the door. Interact with your dog only when he's calm. Ignore the dog until he settles. When he does, call him over to you for quiet hugs and pats.

While your dog may indicate that he needs to go out, barking, jumping, or grabbing you by your shirtsleeve to pull you off your chair is an unacceptable method of doing so. We would not tolerate this behavior from another human being. Why do we allow our dogs to treat us in such a manner?

I worked with a client who had a Border collie that would bark at him incessantly every time he would try to sit down to watch TV. The owner was at his wit's end. His wife simply wanted the dog gone.

To appease the dog and end the barking, the owner would get up and ask the dog what she wanted. He would feed her or play with her. Nothing, it seemed, could console her. She would bark and bark, throwing herself into a frenzy each time he tried to be sensitive to her needs. The duration and the intensity of the barking was more than the family could take. Somehow the owner's behavior—sitting down in the chair—had become the cue for the dog to vocalize, and his attempts to appease her had reinforced and strengthened the behavior. Therefore, the solution was for the owner to change his behavior so that the dog would change hers.

I asked the owner to conduct mini–clicker training sessions from his chair while watching TV. He ignored the barking and reinforced desirable behavior. He clicked and threw treats from his chair for any behavior other than the barking. He clicked and fed her for sitting, standing, or lying down quietly. He clicked and treated her for retrieving items like the TV remote and the car keys. At times, when she would revert back to her old, noisy behavior, he got up and did something else, anything that would take his attention away from the dog's frantic behavior. When the dog quieted, he would return to his chair and continue the clicker training session. Soon, sitting down in his chair became the cue for the dog to either get ready to work or, if not, settle down and curl up near his feet. Be sure that the behavior you want is the behavior you reinforce. Whenever your dog demands that you do something, do something else.

Principle #4: Excuse me!

Dogs are territorial creatures. A common catalyst for biting incidents is when visitors to your home, not realizing the dangerous consequences of their actions, step over the dog if he is lying at the threshold of a room. To avoid this potential scenario, teach your dog to relinquish his space at your or your visitor's request. Having "Excuse Me!" on cue gives your visitors a way to move your dog easily and safely.

Here's how it works in my house: I am in the kitchen about to get a drink of water. Ben is lying down in front of the kitchen sink. Ever so gently I touch my toe to his back leg, trying to encourage him to move. He looks up at me with one sleepy eye. I whip a food treat out of my pocket and toss it a couple of inches from his face. He quickly gets up to get the treat. I click him just as he moves his body away from the area. I toss him another piece of food. I then say "Thank You" because politeness goes both ways.

I do this each time Ben is in a space that I need to be in. As I continue to develop this behavior, I say "Excuse Me!" just before Ben moves his body away. I click for compliance and then shower him with treats.

The finished behavior: Friends are visiting. Ben is lying on the threshold between the dining room and the kitchen. A friend needs to go into the kitchen to get a glass of soda. I tell her to just say "Excuse me!" to Ben and he will move. Sure enough, as she gives Ben the cue, he moves quite readily out of her way. "What nice manners he has!" she exclaims as she proceeds peacefully into the kitchen.

When a dog yields his space to a human, whether it is his owner or a stranger, the behavior demonstrates that the dog understands the structure of the household: he is not the boss. Dogs, in general, can quickly become possessive about spaces such as doorways and sleeping spaces, especially if their owners have coddled them. If you teach the dog to relinquish these spaces at the request of any human, even a temperamentally sensitive dog will acquiesce.

Principle #5: You begin the play, you end the play

It's up to you, not your dog, to decide when it's playtime. Before you begin to play with your dog, ask for a simple behavior such as a sit or down, click for compliance, and then "Let the games begin!" Constructive games like hide-and-seek, soccer, or fetch can add a lot of pleasure to both your lives and become powerful reinforcers for your dog.

Because overstimulation can become aggression in a matter of seconds, I recommend against roughhousing with dogs that have aggression issues of any kind. Keep all games played with your dog gentle and calm. Adults can play tug-of-war with the dog but only under controlled circumstances. Children should never play tug with an aggressive dog, nor should any human whom the dog has ever bitten.

Used in the correct manner, however, tug can be an excellent form of exercise and stress release. If you feel your dog can handle it, ask your dog to sit as the tug toy is being presented. Give a "Take It!" cue and let the game begin. Stay in control of the game by not allowing your dog to whip the toy around his head in a frenzied manner. Instead pull back and forth, in a horizontal line, between owner and dog. After a short game, tell your dog to "Drop it," to let go of the tug toy. If the dog does not know the "Drop it" cue, teach him to let go by trading a small treat for the tug as you say "Drop it." Click as your dog releases the toy. Bring out the tug toy only when you are going to play a game.

How you and your dog play together will affect how your dog plays with the other people in his life, regardless of their age or size. Dogs find playtime with you enormously reinforcing, so take care when and how you allow game playing. Be sure that the timing of the games reinforces only desired behavior.

Principle #6: Your dog's mind needs as much exercise as his body

Many experts stress the need for dogs with aggression problems to have extensive physical exercise. While this is certainly true, I have found that it is just as important to stimulate our dogs mentally. Dogs love to figure things out. They love to use their minds. It is up to us to provide them with exciting mental challenges on a daily basis.

Dogs with aggressive responses especially need to practice making decisions while under stress. We need to be able to provide them with an environment rich in learning opportunities. As they learn new behaviors and their minds expand and become more flexible, their reliance on aggressive behavior to communicate and solve problems will lessen.

Put yourself in your dog's position: You are left alone in the house nine to ten hours a day. You cannot turn on the TV or the radio or read a book. You cannot pick up the phone. You cannot get a bite to eat. All you can do is sleep, walk around the house, sit on the sofa, and look out the window. Your owner has left you with a stuffed animal or squeaky toy, but it gets boring soon. What else can you do? Tear up the rug or chew on the pillows? Get into the garbage?

It's not surprising that when we humans come home at the end of the day, our dogs will do just about anything to get our attention.

Because many of us have no choice but to leave our dogs alone for a number of hours during the day, we need to figure out how to keep them occupied in our absence. Mentally stimulating toys like frozen stuffed Kongs and/or kibble-filled Buster Cubes can make the long, lonely hours of the day more bearable.

To relieve the boredom that household dogs usually experience, owners may send their dogs to doggy daycare, if possible, a couple of times a week or hire a pet sitter to come in several times a day to walk the dog and interact with him. If your dog has an aggression issue you may be limited in your options, which makes clicker training during the hours you are together all the more important.

Clicker training is such a wonderful way to mentally stimulate your dog. It teaches your dog how to think and figure out problems on his own. In this way, he can experiment with his own behavior without fear of a reprimand. Dogs need to learn how to learn and this is best taught by his human caretaker.

Be creative! Teach your dog a variety of neat tricks like "High five!" and "Who's the greatest cook?" Teach him how to retrieve the newspaper or the remote. Teach him how to play soccer with the kids or dance on his hind legs. The sky's the limit with clicker training! (See Creativity, page 65, for more ideas.)

Principle #7: A room of his own

Dogs need a space that they can call their own. Creating a safe space for your dog, whether it is in a crate or in a specific area, will help you manage your dog safely. Your dog needs to learn to trust that, no matter where you put him, it will be a safe environment to which he can retire. Teach your dog to go into his crate and settle peacefully inside, no matter what is happening outside.

If you are going to use a crate, make sure to place it in an area of the house that is well frequented, rather than in the basement or in a secluded part of the house. Your goal is not to isolate your dog from family members but, instead, to help your dog settle down peacefully within an active environment.

Decide which type of crate you would like to purchase. There are some with wire all the way around and some made of plastic that are closed in with a couple of windows to peek through. (Keep in mind that you can cover the wire crate with a blanket should your dog need more privacy.) Either should do fine. If you are unsure of what crate your dog would prefer, borrow a friend's crate to see how well your dog does in it or go to your nearest dog training facility and ask if your dog can try out various crates.

To condition your dog to the crate, feed him in it each day. As your dog goes into the crate to eat, give a cue. "Kennel up!" serves nicely. Shut the door while he is eating and then let him settle for about 30 to 45 minutes after the meal. Do not let him out when he barks or whines, but only when he is quiet.

Whenever you put your dog in the crate, vary the amounts of time and always put in something mentally stimulating for him to do. A frozen stuffed Kong or meaty bone works well. Put your dog in the crate when you are home and sometimes when you are not. Putting your dog in the crate only when you leave the house quickly teaches that going into the crate means that Mom or Dad is leaving him alone. Soon your dog may refuse to go into his crate at all because he knows what happens next.

The wonderful thing about crates is that they make it possible to take your dog's safe space anywhere you go. For example, if your dog is aggressive toward other dogs and you are going to a dog training seminar or an agility match, keep your dog in his crate, in his safe space, until you are ready to interact with him. If your dog is nervous around small children, you can crate him whenever children are in the house. If your dog is anxious around strangers, you can tell him to "kennel up!" whenever the doorbell rings.

Dogs should not be left kenneled for an extreme amount of time. Eight to nine hours a day (an average workday) is simply too long. A doggy daycare or a dog walker can be a great asset to your dog's life if you must be away from home that long every day. To give your dog more space during long periods, you can put up a baby gate to block off an area in your house; condition your dog to this room as you would condition your dog to the crate.

Principle #8: If you give me that, I will give you this

The quickest way to teach a dog to become possessive and defensive when he has something in his mouth is by trying to pry the object away from him. You can, however, teach your dog to eagerly exchange objects with you. Two different scenarios will help illustrate how this works. First imagine this: You have a fifty-dollar bill. I walk up to you and say "Give," and take the fifty-dollar bill out of your hand and walk away. I might give it back to you; then again, I might not. What are you going to do the next time I walk up to you? You are probably going to do one of three things: hide the money, tell me to go away before I actually get to you (dogs do this by growling), or hold it even firmer. Now imagine this: You have your fifty-dollar bill. I walk up to you and give you a hundred-dollar bill in exchange for your fifty dollars. Will you give me the fifty dollars? I bet you will quite willingly. I bet the next time you have fifty dollars you will want me to visit you again.

If you practice mutually beneficial object exchanges with your dog, your dog will always give you items willingly. For dogs with aggressive tendencies, the benefit of object exchanges is that the dogs will not consider humans a threat to whatever they possess. They will begin to love having humans take things away from them so that they might reap the rewards.

Object exchanges are simple to teach. If the dog has an object that you need to take from him, approach him quietly. Click and feed your dog a wonderful treat. As your dog goes to eat the treat, take the object from the dog if it is safe to do so. Click again, tell him "thank you," and give him another handful of treats. Give the object back to him and repeat the exercise if you are able. Do make sure that the treat that you offer the dog matches the reinforcement value of the object that he has in his mouth.

Never chase your dog into a tight space (under a piece of furniture, for example) or grab him by the collar to get the object back. Doing so can greatly increase the risk of getting bitten.

Principle #9:   Limit your dog's access to his toys

Keep your dog's toys in a special place where he cannot freely access them. Offer your dog a "new" toy only after he performs a familiar behavior for you. Click the correct behavior and give your dog the toy he earned. Pick up all your dog's toys at the end of the day. Rotate them on a day-by-day basis so that your dog will not tire of seeing the same toys over and over again and you won't need to buy a steady stream of new toys to keep his interest.

Keep all interactive toys, like tennis balls and Frisbees, out of the dog's reach until it is time for you to play with him. Remember, the game begins when you decide that you want to play and only after your dog performs a desired behavior for you.

Principle #10: The bowl is the cue to eat

When your dog sees his food bowl he knows it's time to eat. Feed your dog twice a day (three times a day for puppies) and pick up the food bowl after each meal, regardless of whether or not it is empty. Dogs should not be allowed to eat whenever they feel like it. This is not good for their metabolism nor does it promote a healthy handler/dog relationship.

Before you feed your dog, ask your dog for a simple behavior and click when he performs the behavior. Give your dog his meal as his reward. We want our dogs to know that being fed is not to be taken for granted. As we need to work for our meals, dogs should too.

CHAPTER 2

Laying the Groundwork: Foundation Behaviors

The foundation behaviors form the core of the obedience behaviors that your dog will need to know before you expose him to the stressful environments and encounters in which he tends to display aggression. Once he knows these behaviors and is confident in performing them, any one of them may serve as an incompatible, alternate behavior that you can request from your dog to head off a situation in which he might become aggressive.

Teaching your dog these behaviors—from eye contact and loose leash walking to recall and holding an object in his mouth—will help you remain in control of your dog in any setting, so that you can teach him the skills he needs to interact politely with others. Courteous canines are welcomed in many more places than "out of control" dogs, who end up having narrow lives because their owners have neither the strength nor the desire to take them anywhere.

I've presented the steps to training these behaviors in a recipe format. Most are very simple and straightforward, if you understand how to break the training down into its smallest parts. These "recipes" take you through that process.

At the top of each recipe, the behavior—your training goal—is defined. Following is a section called *"Especially helpful when…"* This section provides examples of why this behavior is so important to teach, as well as in what circumstances it can be used effectively. *"How to make it happen"* breaks the training down into steps. The last section of each recipe, *"Secrets of success,"* gives tips that will help you and your dog reach this particular behavioral goal and avoid common mistakes. Later chapters contain additional training recipes for behaviors targeted at healing your dog's aggression.

Proper Equipment

Before you begin to teach your dog any of the behaviors, read each recipe carefully, from start to finish, and make sure that you have the proper equipment at hand. Additional information on these training tools can be found in the Resources section at the end of this book, page 179.

Clickers

A clicker is a device that makes a sharp distinctive sound; clickers now come in many colors, shapes, and sizes. If your dog is noise-sensitive, consider using a type of clicker that produces a quieter sound, or even the button on the top of a ballpoint pen.

Leashes

A six-foot leather or web leash is recommended for all of the exercises; choose whichever is most comfortable for you to hold. No flexi-leads or chain leashes, please.

Collars

A head collar is best. There are three main types of head collars: the Gentle Leader, the Halti, and the Snoot Loop. All of the collars work with the same basic premise: they allow you to control the dog's head, which makes it possible to control the dog's body. Proper use of one of these devices allows you to maintain control of your dog at all times.

Experiment with each of the collars so that you can determine which one your dog will feel most comfortable in. (You may be able to borrow some from friends, or take your dog into a pet store and try on a few there.) Take time to desensitize your dog to the collar before beginning your training program (see page 88, Touching/Grabbing Your Dog's Collar, to learn how to do this). If your dog is unable to wear a head collar, then you can use a harness that fits comfortably around his chest and shoulders.

Muzzles

If your dog has bitten a person or another dog, and you must do some of your training in the presence of other people or dogs, you will need to purchase a muzzle. As you work through your dog's rehabilitation program, keeping everyone safe, at all times, is of paramount importance.

Muzzles come in three different materials: nylon, basket, or leather. Each type can be used effectively as long as the muzzle is intact and fitted properly. The muzzle should fit over your dog's snout sufficiently so that he cannot open his mouth enough to inflict injury, but can still eat treats. As with the head halter, you will need to desensitize your dog to the muzzle before having him wear it during a training session.

Bait Bag

You will need a pouch to keep your dog's training treats in while you are out and about. You'll want to maintain a high rate of reinforcement—feed your dog lots and lots of small treats—so be sure that you can get your fingers in and out of the bag easily while walking and holding the leash.

Target Stick

This is a stick that you teach your dog to touch the end of on cue. Though there are many fancy target sticks that you can buy, you can also use common, everyday items such as rulers, dowels, and pointers.

Long Line

A nylon line is available at any hardware store and can usually be cut to any length. You can secure it to your dog's collar with a metal clasp, similar to the clasp on a leash, or just tie the line to your dog's leash.

Preliminary Requirements for Training Sessions

When teaching your dog the foundation behaviors, you should start in a quiet room without distractions. Attach your six-foot leash to your dog's collar and have a clicker and tasty treats in your hand. As your dog's behavior becomes more reliable, you will begin to increase the distraction level of the environment in which you are working.

It is important to practice these behaviors on-leash as well as off-leash. You need to know beforehand in which hand you will hold your leash, and in which hand you will hold the clicker. And you will have to practice clicking and dispensing the training treats at a high rate of reinforcement. Doing all these maneuvers while watching your dog interact with his environment can feel awkward at first, but it gets easier with practice. Remember that when you feel your dog is ready to try out his trained behaviors in settings where he has previously been aggressive, you will need your body to know what to do even if your mind is consumed with your own stress.

Training Tips

Successful training sessions rely on several factors. Having the following elements in place before you begin will help ensure success. First, choose your treats. You want your treats to be eaten quickly so that you can reinforce again, but also so that your dog doesn't chew so long that he has time to fixate on his environment. You need to be able to click and feed quickly and keep moving to maintain control of your dog in stressful settings. Squeezable cheese in tubes or cans, or the canned pastes from the Kong company, are great alternatives for reinforcing a dog that is wearing a muzzle. The treats should be highly desirable—bits of greasy hotdog, small chunks of cheese or turkey/chicken, or dried liver—that your dog doesn't usually get to enjoy in the course of his day or regular meals. The higher the perceived value of the treats, the harder your dog will work to obtain them.

- Prepare a dish or bag of tasty rewards. Training treats should be a "soft" food your dog can swallow quickly and easily.

- Use an extremely high rate of reinforcement when training a new behavior. Click and feed the heck out of your dog. Frequent reinforcement keeps your dog focused on you and keeps his adrenaline levels lower.

- Use treats equal to the level of distraction in which you are working. For example, bring something highly palatable to places where it might be difficult to get the desired behavior. Use a less reinforcing treat when performing easier behaviors at a place where the dog is used to working—at home, for example.

- Break up behavior into separate components and teach each component separately. Teaching behavior in small steps leads to more learning at a faster rate. The recipes that follow will help you to do this.

- Training sessions should be kept short, especially when beginning any new behavior. Three to five minutes per session is adequate, and sometimes even that might be lengthy.

- When working on a new level of criteria, temporarily relax the old ones. This means the first few times you click and reward your dog for a new aspect of a particular behavior, don't worry if other aspects of that behavior aren't perfect. For example, if you have trained your dog to make eye contact while sitting and facing you in your living room, and out in the dog park he sits facing you with intermittent eye contact, reward him for accomplishing at least part of the behavior in this new, stressful environment.

- Expect newly learned behaviors to fall apart temporarily in new environments. In every new setting, take your dog back to "kindergarten" and reinforce the small steps toward your training goal until your dog attains his previous level of behavior in the new environment.

- During a training session, give 100 percent attention to your dog so that you can observe the smallest behaviors—or lack of behavior—and click and reward it. In treating aggression, you frequently may click and reward the absence of displays of aggression, and you'll need a sharp, attentive eye to catch those moments.

- When your dog is heavily stressed, shape behavior in small increments. If your dog explodes into an aggressive display, you may have gone too far, too fast.

- Keep a training journal. It is very helpful to keep track of your dog's training progress and to write down your thoughts as you move through this sometimes frustrating journey.

- Vary the reinforcers you use while working with your dog. Sometimes a click equals a treat. Sometimes it equals petting or praise. Or your reward may be a game of fetch or a walk outside. Keep your dog surprised, and thus focused on you rather than on potential targets for aggression.

- Don't feed your dog a big meal just before a training session. Of course we should never starve our dogs, but an appetite is a powerful motivator.

- Exercise your dog before you conduct his training session in a stressful environment. Some dogs benefit by heavy exercise before exposure to situations they find stressful. A tired dog is less likely to seek a confrontation.

- Read all the steps of a training recipe before working with your dog, making sure that you understand the goal. You'll want to recognize the behavior when the dog accomplishes it.

- If possible, bring a friend or family member along with you when you are working with your dog outdoors. It's helpful to have an extra set of hands to hold treats, the leash, and other equipment. He or she can also help you to keep the environment safe, for example by warding off another dog from approaching. In some exercises, you'll need a cooperative friend with a dog that your dog knows and, if possible, is comfortable with.

Training Recipes: Foundation Behaviors

Eye Contact

Follow these steps to teach your dog to look at your face immediately when you say "Watch" or "Look."

Especially helpful when…

- You are in an environment that your dog considers dangerous and uncomfortable. He must be ready to give you his full attention, no matter the circumstance, so that you can help him focus and read your cues for appropriate behavior. Steady eye contact with you gives your dog comfort and guidance when he most needs it.

How to make it happen:

1. Prepare your treats and stand in a quiet room with your dog. Then wait.
2. Each time your dog lifts his head and/or turns his body toward you, click and treat. Watch for and reward even subtle movements toward you: a lean, a shift in the shoulders, and so on. Soon your dog will begin to look at your face in anticipation of another click and treat.
3. When your dog begins to look at you repeatedly, click and treat him for direct eye contact only.
4. As your dog continues to make eye contact, introduce a verbal cue, "Watch," or "Look," immediately before the behavior occurs.
5. Click and treat when he performs the behavior only after you've given the cue.
6. Take your dog to different locations to generalize this behavior. Pack your dog, leash, clicker, and treats into your car and go on your errands. Make sure your treats are extra delicious! Repeat Steps 1 through 3 at every new location.

Luring Eye Contact

Some dogs are reluctant to look into the face of anyone, including their owners. If your dog seems excessively shy about eye contact, you might want to use the luring method to get the behavior started.

How to make it happen:

1. Show your dog the treat by putting it in front of his nose.
2. Slowly raise the treat to your eyes in one long, drawn-out motion. As you do this, say your cue word very slowly ("L—o—o—k") as you bring the treat up toward your eyes.
3. As your dog looks up at you, click and feed your dog.
4. Continue Steps 1 through 3 until your dog begins feeling more comfortable looking up into your face.
5. Continue to work this behavior in new situations and different environments.

Automatic Eye Contact (in the presence of stressful elements)

If your dog is afraid or uncomfortable with a particular event or element—other dogs, passing joggers, children in strollers—the appearance of that stimulus may become the cue itself for your dog to automatically turn and look at you. Then you can request behavior incompatible with an aggressive display.

How to make it happen:

1. Take your dog to an environment where he will see the questionable stimulus or event from a distance. Stay at a sufficient distance from the stimulus to prevent your dog from reacting aggressively to it.
2. Click and feed your dog quickly for looking at and hearing (if applicable) the event or element he fears. Work quickly and do not let your dog fixate on the stimulus. As you continue to work this behavior, your dog will turn from looking at the

thing that frightens him to looking at you in anticipation of the click and treat. Click this moment and give your dog a handful of treats!

3. Click and feed your dog for eye contact whenever he is exposed to the undesirable stimulus or events.

Secrets of success:

- Do not try to physically force your dog to look at you, no matter how stressful the situation might be.
- Allow your dog to look at the aversive stimulus before giving you eye contact.
- Teach your dog to look at your face on a verbal cue, as well as in the presence of the aversive stimuli or events. This cue needs to be powerful so that it can interrupt inappropriate behavior before it begins.
- Reinforce your dog any time he gives you eye contact, whether or not you asked for it. You want your dog to find you intensely interesting!

Sit

Follow these steps to teach your dog to sit reliably in any environment.

Especially helpful when...

- Your dog is faced with an unfamiliar situation. If you ask him to sit, this will occupy him so he will be distracted from possible stressors; he will be too busy following your command to lunge aggressively at another dog or person, for example. Coupled with eye contact and stay behavior, this is a very effective strategy for defusing potentially dangerous situations.

How to make it happen:

1. Capture the behavior: click and throw a treat on the floor every time your dog folds into a sit. Or lure the behavior: take a piece of food and hold it just above

your dog's nose. As he starts to sniff the treat, slowly bring the treat back over his head. As you tilt his head back, his hind end will plunk into a sit. Click and feed the dog just as his rear end hits the floor.

2. Repeat these exercises several times until your dog sits readily.

3. As your dog begins to sit automatically, add the verbal cue "Sit" right before the behavior occurs.

4. Practice this behavior in a variety of environments and situations.

Secrets of success:

•   While putting the behavior on cue, say your cue word once and then help your dog perform the behavior. Do not ask your dog to sit five times before you decide to help him out.

•   If you and your dog are in a stressful environment, ask your dog to sit instead of asking him to down. Until your dog gets used to performing behaviors in an aversive environment, the sit position will come much more easily than the submissive posture of the down. Your dog already feels uncomfortable; trying to make him perform the down behavior (when a sit will suffice) will only increase his stress level (and yours).

•   Never physically force your dog into the sit position.

Down

The following steps will help you teach your dog to lie down in any situation or environment. Please note that the down position is a more submissive posture; your dog will probably find it more difficult to assume this position in a threatening or stressful environment. Because of this, the reliability of the behavior might be affected by the situation.

Especially helpful when…

- You see another dog and handler walking down the street. Instead of allowing your dog to growl and lunge forward, give your dog the cue to lie down and wait patiently as they walk by.
- A jogger is running toward you and your dog as you are out for your midday stroll. Previously, your dog has lunged out and bitten a jogger on the hand. Wanting to avoid another disaster, you give your dog the cue to lie down as the jogger runs safely past.

How to make it happen:

1. Capture the behavior: click and treat your dog every time he lies down.
2. Or lure the behavior: ask your dog to sit.
3. Take a piece of food and keep it at your dog's nose without allowing him to eat it.
4. Let your dog's nose follow the treat as you bring it, in a straight line, down to the floor.
5. As the dog continues to sniff the treat, slowly pull the food out along the floor.
6. Gently guide the dog into the down position.
7. Click as the dog's elbows get closer to the floor.
8. Feed the dog and repeat the previous steps until your dog lies down readily.
9. Because of the submissive posture of the down position, some dogs find it difficult to lie down automatically. Be patient. Click and reward your dog at incremental positions as his body gets closer to the floor. Eventually the dog will lie down completely.
10. Repeat Steps 1 or 2 until your dog lies down easily.
11. Add the verbal cue "Down" right before the behavior occurs.
12. Practice this behavior in a variety of environments and situations until it is reliable.

Secrets of success:

- While putting the behavior on cue, say your cue word once and then help your dog perform the behavior. Do not ask your dog to lie down five times before you decide to help him out.

- Take note of where your dog hesitates to perform this behavior reliably on cue and work especially in those situations or environments until he feels comfortable executing the behavior. In the meantime, ask your dog to sit in these situations instead.
- Never physically force your dog into the down position.

Heeling on a Loose Leash

Your dog must be able to walk with you on a loose leash no matter the environment or situation. Pulling on the leash is a very common canine behavior problem, especially when a dog is stressed.

Especially helpful when…

- You want to take your dog on a long walk or run in order to exercise him properly.
- You need to maintain physical control of your dog, especially when exposing him to new situations or events that he might find stressful.
- You need to teach your dog that you are his leader, and that you don't want him to drag you around at the end of his leash.

How to make it happen:

1. Place your dog on your left, with a six-foot leash attached to his collar. (The traditional placement is on the left, but feel free to place your dog on your right, if that is more comfortable for you.)
2. Hold the leash in your right hand (or left hand, if your dog is on your right) with the clicker pressed up against the bunched leash. The leash will now hang loosely in front of your body. This leaves your left hand free to feed your dog in heel position.
3. Have your treats in an easy-to-reach pouch. They should be plentiful and palatable.
4. Take one step. Click and treat your dog for stepping with you.
5. Take another step. Click and feed. Try another step. Click and feed, if your dog progresses with you. With each step, click and treat your dog for keeping pace with you.

6. If your dog should pull forward, freeze in your tracks and begin walking backward slowly. As the dog slows back to your pace, begin to walk forward, clicking and feeding the dog for remaining by your side. (For especially energetic pullers, freeze, turn 180 degrees, and start walking in the other direction. Click and feed the dog as he catches up and stays close by your side.)

7. Slowly increase the number of steps you can take without your dog pulling you forward. Click and feed every two steps, three steps, four steps, and so on.

8. As your dog starts to understand that he needs to stay close and keep pace with you, gradually introduce distractions by walking outside, near other people, and near other dogs. Whenever you work in a new environment and increase the level of potential distractions, repeat Steps 4 through 6.

Secrets of success:

• Maintain a high rate of reinforcement when your dog is walking nicely by your side.

• Feed your dog quickly after each click.

• If you have chosen to use a head collar, be sure that your dog feels comfortable in it. If he is uneasy and keeps trying to get it off, desensitize him to the collar before proceeding (see page 88).

• When beginning, keep the leash short so the dog doesn't have a lot of space in which to pull away from you.

• Never allow your dog to pull you. If he succeeds even once in a while, you are inadvertently employing what trainers call "a variable ratio schedule of reinforcement," a method of occasional rewards that can make a behavior stronger and much more difficult to eradicate.

• Practice this exercise until it is very reliable before asking your dog to perform it in situations in which he has previously felt stressed or displayed aggression.

Targeting

When your dog knows how to touch an object such as a target stick, on cue, you can use this behavior in a variety of situations. You can also teach your dog to touch your hand as his "target."

Especially helpful when…

- Your dog is afraid of a certain item. If you train your dog to touch the item, his focus on the training cue (and on earning a click and a reward) may outweigh his fear of the item.
- Your dog is timid when people come to the house to visit. Teach your dog to target visitors' fists or shoes so that when they come in he has a job to focus on, and a reward to earn for doing so.
- Your dog is nervous at the veterinarian's office. Ask your dog to target your hand as he is getting weighed, having his temperature taken, or getting his nails clipped.
- You need to distract your dog from a passing dog. Ask him to target your hand as you hold it in the opposite direction.

How to make it happen:

1. Hold the object, or target stick, in your hand.
2. Click and feed your dog every time he looks at the stick or touches it. (If he is uninterested, rub a piece of hotdog or a piece of cheese on the tip of the stick. Click and feed him as he sniffs the baited spot. Repeat this several times.)
3. Now present the stick without any enticement.
4. Click and feed your dog for touching the stick.
5. Once your dog is repeatedly touching the stick, then add a verbal cue.
6. Make the behavior more challenging as you move the stick to locations that make it harder for your dog to touch it. For example, teach your dog to touch the stick when you hold it to the left of his head, to the right of his head, above and below

his head, under a chair, and so on.

7. Once the dog is touching the stick reliably, ask the dog to follow the stick. Here's how to accomplish this step:

   - Hold the stick a step away from the dog's nose.
   - Click and treat as your dog moves forward to touch the end of the stick.
   - Now hold the stick a little farther away.
   - Click and feed your dog as he takes several steps forward to touch the end of the stick.
   - With success, slowly increase the distance at which your dog will follow the stick.

8. Once your dog is following the stick successfully, be creative! Have him follow the stick over things, like a jump, and under things, like a chair.

9. Continue to make it a challenging game.

Secrets of success:

- Hold the stick out for a few seconds, and if your dog is not interested immediately, put the stick behind your back and try again. Do rub a piece of tantalizing food on the tip of the stick just to get the behavior going.
- You can follow the same sequence for any object that you want your dog to touch.

Stay

A reliable sit/stay or down/stay is a primary tool to be used to prevent aggressive episodes. Your dog must learn to stay in either the sit or down position regardless of your position or the setting. Reliability is the key. Please note that dogs with fear issues are not likely to perform a stay easily, especially in a down position, in a stressful environment. Practice the stay behavior in the sit position first, and as the dog becomes more comfortable, begin to work in the down position.

Especially helpful when…

- You have arrived at a dog training class. You need to take your coat off, get the treats ready, and put your sneakers on. No matter which way you turn or how long it may take, your dog will be patiently sitting and waiting for you rather than focusing on stressors within the environment.

- You arrive at a park where children and other dogs are running and playing. You must prepare your leash, treats, and other supplies before you enter the park, and want your dog to stay calmly at your side while you do.

How to make it happen:

1. Ask your dog to sit or down.

2. Tell your dog to stay either by giving the cue verbally or by holding up the palm of your hand about six inches from the dog's nose.

3. Once he is in position, count to five. Click and feed your dog for staying in either the sit or down position for five seconds. Remember that the click ends the behavior, so if your dog gets up after the click, it is fine. Make sure to give the "Stay" cue again, before continuing. Make sure your dog remained in whichever position you originally asked him for.

4. Slowly lengthen the time you are asking your dog to remain in position. Work in increments of seconds at first. Slowly increase to minutes.

5. Work on each piece of criteria separately:
   - distance (how far you are from your dog)
   - duration (how long the dog is to remain in position)
   - distractions (your dog stays, perfectly still, no matter what is happening around him)

6. Once your dog is staying for at least 30 seconds, practice getting him to stay under different conditions. Click and treat your dog while you are sitting, standing,

lying down, standing with your back to the dog, putting your coat on, tying your shoe, looking for your car keys in your purse or coat, getting out your treats, looking up at the ceiling, and so on. Work on as many positions as you can think of, so that your dog understands that "stay" means "stay," no matter where you are or what you are doing.

7. Now that your dog is getting more reliable, start practicing this skill in several different locations. Remember to "go back to kindergarten" initially in each new environment, and to work on one criterion (distance, duration, or distractions) at a time.

8. As your dog continues to progress, you can start asking your dog to stay while you walk one step away, two steps, and so forth.

9. To build your dog's confidence, ask him to stay with his back to a variety of distractions, for example, kids, other dogs, traffic, etc.

10. Please note that if your dog is an aggressive dog, you should never leave him unattended in a public area, no matter how reliable his "stay" behavior is.

Secrets of success:

• Be consistent! When you ask your dog to perform a specific behavior, make sure your dog does just that. For example, if you are working on a sit/stay and your dog sinks into the down position, cue your dog to sit again, and get him back up on his feet by walking toward him. *Never pull him up by the collar or scruff.* (Remember, learning principles are the same for dogs as for humans: aggression begets aggression. If you show a dog aggressive behavior then you will, more than likely, get it back in some form or fashion.) Again ask for a sit. If your dog is confused, go back to page 40 and reread the Sit recipe and page 41 to reread the Down section. Advance when your dog's behavior is more reliable. The same rules apply when working on the down position. The dog must do whatever behavior you asked for. Inconsistency reduces reliability in highly distracting environments.

- Click and feed at the end of the stay behavior only.
- If you would like to split up a longer duration of stay behavior (five minutes, for example), click and feed your dog for a set time (three minutes, let's say) and then tell your dog to stay again, either by using your verbal cue or with a hand signal. Click and feed for completed behavior. This method is more sound than haphazardly feeding treats in the middle of the behavior without the click, a practice that can become very confusing to the dog and eventually can cause undue stress as well as potentially unreliable behavior.
- Vary the duration of the behavior.

Recall

Your dog should come directly to you when you call him, regardless of environment or circumstances. This behavior may be one of the most important that you will ever teach your dog.

Especially helpful when…

- You want to call your dog back to you to interrupt play behavior that has gotten out of hand.
- You are walking your dog off-leash in the woods. From a distance, you see youngsters walking their dog. Fearing your overexuberant dog will run and jump on them, you call him back to you so that you can put him back on his leash.
- You want to let your dog run off-leash at the beach so that you might exercise him properly. You need to be sure that your dog will come back to you when he's called.

How to make it happen:

Here are five ways to strengthen the recall.

I. Random Recalls

1. Keep your clicker with you at all times.
2. Scatter little containers of treats in every room in the house.
3. Anytime your dog comes to you when you call, click.
4. Put your hand on his collar, ask him to sit, and give him a treat; always secure your dog before you give him his reward so that he does not learn to come when called, eat his treat, and take off again.
5. If you call your dog and he does not come, bend down, throw your arms wide, and call him enthusiastically. Click and feed him as he comes to you. Or try taking a couple of steps backward as an extra "enticement" cue.
6. Practice this exercise indoors as well as outdoors in a safe, enclosed space.

II. Flying Fronts

1. Work with your dog in a quiet room without distractions.
2. Hold the clicker and treats in your hand.
3. Show the dog the treat and throw it a couple of feet away from you.
4. As your dog goes to eat the treat, call him and take several steps backward.
5. Click as your dog happily comes to you.
6. Ask your dog to sit.
7. Hold the dog's collar while you feed him his treat.
8. When your dog is coming to you reliably, start to throw the treat farther and farther away.
9. Change the environment that you are working in, gradually increasing the distractions.

III. Traditional Obedience Recall

1. Work with your dog in a quiet room without distractions.

2. Hold the clicker and treats in your hand.

3. Ask your dog to sit and stay.

4. Walk a couple of feet away from your dog.

5. Turn and face him. (He should still be staying.)

6. Call your dog to you.

7. Click as he starts to move toward you.

8. Ask your dog to sit.

9. Hold the dog's collar while you feed him his treat. (As your dog is coming toward you, you can either meet him halfway, ask for the sit, and give him his treat—a good technique for beginner dogs—or, you can wait until he comes all the way to you before asking for the sit and giving him his reward.)

10. When your dog is coming to you reliably, gradually increase the distance that you walk away from your dog.

11. Work in different environments, gradually increasing the distraction level.

IV. Hide-and-Seek Indoors (great fun with kids!)

1. Have someone hold the dog in one room of the house.

2. Hide in another room.

3. Call your dog.

4. When he finds you, click, ask him to sit, hold his collar, and give him his treat.

5. As your dog becomes more experienced at this game, hide in harder-to-discover places. Then take the game outside to a safe, enclosed environment.

V. "Ping Pong" Recall

1. Arm two or three friends with clickers and your dog's favorite treats.

2. One by one, take turns calling the dog, using whatever word you have chosen to be your recall cue.

3. When the dog comes to the person who called, have the person click, ask the dog to sit, hold the dog's collar, and give a delicious treat.

4. As the dog gets more skilled, spread yourselves farther and farther apart.

5. Begin playing this game in the house and then move it to a quiet, safe area outside.

6. Gradually increase distance and distractions.

Secrets of success:

- Always click and give the dog a reward for coming to you, regardless of whether or not you called him.

- Mix and match the exercises above to teach a highly reliable recall.

- Practice the behavior using each of the following criteria:
  - Come from across the room.
  - Come from another room.
  - Come no matter who calls.
  - Come now.
  - Come, even if engaged in another activity such as drinking water, eating a meal, or playing with another dog.

- Vary your reinforcers; a favorite toy, a treat, a game, petting, or praise all work well here.

- If the behavior is not yet reliable, attach a long line to your dog's collar for added safety.

- Never call your dog to you to punish him.

- Never call your dog to you to do an unpleasant task such as clipping his nails or cleaning his ears; go and get him.

- Practice the recall behavior in a variety of environments, gradually increasing the distraction level.

- Do not allow your dog off-leash until his recall behavior is reliable.

Four on the Floor

No jumping allowed! Teach your dog this behavior and he will greet everyone that comes into the house, family members and visitors alike, in a polite and controlled manner with his four feet on the floor.

Especially helpful when...

- Your dog barks and jumps when strangers enter the house. Rather than allowing your dog to jump up on your guests, teach him to accept the arrival of your visitors calmly. The effort of keeping his four feet on the floor may reduce other threatening postures and vocalizations. Make sure your dog has on his Gentle Leader head collar so that you remain in control. (If your dog has shown aggression toward humans, muzzle him when practicing this exercise with visitors.)

How to make it happen:

1. Stand completely still. At first, do not move your arms and legs. The quieter your body signals stay, the quieter your dog's body signals will be.
2. Click and feed your dog only when all four of his feet remain on the floor, regardless of what body position he is actually in. (You are clicking for the absence of the jumping-up behavior.)
   - Click, even if it is only to mark a second of the desired behavior, and feed.
   - Throw the treat on the floor. Instead of dropping the treat right beside you, throw the treat away from you so that your dog has to get up and walk to get the treat, and then return to you to repeat the behavior.
   - If your dog's feet remain on the floor as he is walking toward you, quickly click and throw another treat.
3. Repeat ten times, then end the session.
4. If your dog should jump up on you at any point during the session, simply cross your arms and turn your back. Ignore the behavior. If you are physically unable

to do this, you might start working this behavior with your dog's leash tethered to an eye hook in the wall. (If you do this, please make sure that the leash is fastened to your dog's flat buckle collar, not to the Gentle Leader.) With the dog's leash tethered to the hook, if your dog begins jumping, you can simply walk out of the room and ignore your dog until he quiets down.

5. As you continue clicking and feeding your dog for not jumping up, gradually add the following criteria to your training sessions:

   • Move your arms. Click and treat for no jumping.

   • Move your legs. Click and treat for no jumping.

   • Start walking slowly. Click and throw the food on the floor with each successful step.

   • Begin to walk faster.

   • Start to add more distracting body movements; for example, do jumping jacks, march in place, or clap your hands.

6. Now that your dog is remaining down with more distractions and for longer periods, add a visitor.

7. Repeat Steps 2 through 5.

8. If you feel it is safe to do so, have the visitor be the one who clicks and treats the dog for proper behavior.

Secrets of success:

• Remember, dogs love a reaction! Jumping up on people is especially reinforcing because they always get a reaction, whether it's a pat or a screech and a push. Attention, whether positive or negative, keeps a behavior strong.

• If visitors are coming and you won't have time to use the visit as a "Four on the Floor" teaching opportunity, put your dog in his crate or a separate room to prevent giving him the chance to jump on your visitors.

• Teach your dog a behavior incompatible with jumping up. For example, if you have a dog that naturally retrieves, teach your dog to run to get his toy every time a visitor comes to the door. You can also teach your dog to go to his safe space when he hears a knock on the door or the ring of the doorbell.

- Each time your dog begins to jump up, ask him to sit and help him to perform this behavior. Click and feed him when he is in the sit position.

- When training any behavior, have your sessions in areas of the house that may be stressful or stimulating for your dog: doorways, the kitchen, or in rooms the dog is not usually allowed. Doing so will help your dog to learn self-control.

Kennel Up When Visitors Arrive

Once you've taught your dog this behavior, he will run to his safe space (usually a crate) when visitors ring your doorbell or knock.

Especially helpful when...

- Your dog is aggressive to visitors. The cue for the behavior is a knock at the door or ringing of the doorbell; hearing this, your dog will quickly run to his safe space. You can then secure him while you welcome your guests and until the situation (and your dog) has calmed down enough so that your dog is able to greet your guests without being aggressive.

How to make it happen:

1. Put your crate in a quiet room without distractions.
2. Have your clicker and treats ready.
3. Before proceeding, make sure your dog already knows how to go into his kennel on cue (see "A room of his own," page 25).
4. Decide to which new cue, the doorbell ring or the knock on the door, you would like your dog to respond.

5. While you are teaching this behavior, ask expected visitors to not use the sound to which you are training the dog. For example, if you are going to teach your dog to go into his crate when he hears the doorbell, have visitors enter without ringing the doorbell.

6. Decide how you are going to produce the new go-to-your-crate cue readily. For example, if you are going to use a ringing sound, it might be handy to either purchase a remote control for your doorbell or tape-record your doorbell ringing at various intervals. You can also use a bike bell or a desk bell.

7. Give the new cue, e.g., one ring or a knock on the door or another wooden surface.

8. Give the original go-to-your-crate cue.

9. Click and feed the dog for entering his crate.

10. Repeat Steps 7 through 9 until the dog moves quickly into his crate at the cue of a ring or a knock.

11. Now begin to lengthen the time between when the new cue is given and when the original cue is given.
    - Present the ring or knock.
    - Wait to see if the dog will enter the crate. (Click and feed any interest in the crate at all.)
    - If the dog needs help, give the dog the original cue.
    - Click and feed for compliance.

12. Gradually begin to fade the old cue, by making it less and less obvious, while giving more emphasis to the new cue.

13. Continue working the behavior until the response to the new cue is just as strong as the old.

14. Now plan several practice sessions.
    - Have a friend come to the door and ring the bell once. (Do not have your friend actually open the door.)

- Encourage your dog to go to his crate. (Back up the new cue with the original cue if needed.)
- Continue to practice these repetitions until the behavior is reliable.

15. Once the behavior is reliable, increase the distraction level.

- Have one person ring the bell and begin to open the door.
- Now the person can actually come in.
- Work up to several people coming in quietly.
- Have one person come in making lots of noise, etc.

Secrets of success:

- Make sure your original signal to tell your dog to go to his safe space is reliable before you transfer the behavior to a new cue. The learning process will go much faster this way.
- If, by mistake, the sound is heard (the doorbell, for example) and your behavior is not yet complete, escort your dog into his crate on your original cue. Do not let the visitor in until your dog is safely secured.
- Do not ever let your dog ambush people at the door. Before visitors arrive either put your dog in his crate or leash him before the door is opened. Do not let him rehearse the behavior; this will only serve to reinforce it.

Leave It

After you've taught your dog this behavior, you'll be able to ask him to ignore an object he finds enticing or walk away from a potentially aggression-eliciting encounter or situation.

Especially helpful when…

- A child, holding an ice cream cone, comes running up to you and your dog.

Although your dog is nervous around small children, the enticement of the ice cream is too hard to resist. Rather than allowing your dog to lunge in an attempt to grab the ice cream cone, you tell your dog to "leave it."

- You are walking your dog on a trail in the woods when another dog comes by carrying a stick. Your dog, wanting what the other dog has, begins to pull you toward the other dog. You tell your dog to "leave it" and keep walking.

- You are in an obedience class and another dog threatens your dog. You tell your dog to "leave it" and move on to the next exercise.

How to make it happen:

1. Work with your dog in a quiet room without distractions.

2. Put an enticing treat in one of your hands.

3. Show the dog the treat in your hand but don't let him get it.

4. In front of your dog, close the hand that is holding the treat and make a fist.

5. Present your fist for your dog to sniff.

6. Click and treat your dog for backing away from your hand. If your dog sniffs and nudges your hand, ignore the behavior. When he stops sniffing and moves his head away, click and open your hand so that the dog can eat his reward.

7. Repeat the previous steps several times until your dog no longer sniffs your hand and immediately backs away.

8. Once your dog performs Step 7 reliably, attach the verbal cue "Leave it!" before he moves away.

9. Put a treat on the floor. Make sure your dog knows it's there.

10. Stand close to the treat, with your foot ready to cover it should your dog decide to take it on his own. Wait.

11. If your dog moves toward the treat, lightly cover it with your foot so that it is inaccessible.

12. If your dog moves away from the treat, click and allow your dog to eat it.

13. Repeat the previous steps until your dog is readily moving away from the exposed treat.

14. Once he is performing Step 13 reliably, then attach the verbal cue "Leave It!" as he moves away from the treat.

15. Generalize the behavior to other objects such as toys, tennis balls, and sticks.

16. Work in different environments with different sets of distractions. Be creative. Make the game as challenging as it can be. Here are a couple of examples:

   • Put treats on the floor (start with one and slowly graduate to two, three, and so on) and heel your dog around them. Do not let your dog eat any treats off of the floor. Click and feed your dog from your hand for compliance. Eventually you will be able to click and tell your dog to clean up the floor as a jackpot reward, or heel your dog to each treat individually, and on your release cue, let him eat the treats one by one.

   • Work on a sit/stay, stand/stay, or down/stay with a treat out in front of your dog and tell him to "Leave it." Once the exercise is complete, click and tell your dog to "Take it!"

Secrets of success:

• If your dog is having trouble leaving the treat initially, use a treat of a lesser reinforcement value such as a piece of kibble or a Cheerio. As your dog becomes more successful with the exercise, heighten the reinforcement value of the object.

• Once your dog starts leaving a variety of different objects, begin to click and treat your dog for leaving other "things" such as dogs, fast-moving objects, etc. Practice with these just as you would practice with any other object.

Hold an Object

With this recipe, you teach your dog to hold an object in his mouth for a set length of time. He learns to take it on cue and release it when asked. (Please note that some breeds of dogs, retrievers for example, will find it inherently rewarding to carry an object in their mouths. For them, this skill might be easier to learn. It does not mean, however, that other breeds of dogs cannot be taught to hold an object happily.) The beauty of this exercise is that once your dog gets used to walking with this specific object in his mouth, it may evolve into a "pacifier" of sorts that he will voluntarily pick up and carry whenever he feels nervous.

Especially helpful when…

* You are walking your dog in an area saturated with other dogs. Your dog's job is to carry his object while he is walking in this environment. While he is concentrating on holding the object in his mouth, he will be less likely to focus on anything else. Make sure that other people and dogs respect his space and do not try to take the toy away from him.
* Some dogs, while they hold a toy in their mouth, do not jump up. When you hear the doorbell ring, give your dog his toy, and allow him to carry it to the door to meet the newcomers.

How to make it happen:

1. Decide what object you will want your dog to hold. Choose an object that your dog will feel comfortable carrying in his mouth for an extended length of time, such as a favorite stuffed animal or a tennis ball.
2. Start in a quiet room without distractions.
3. Have your clicker and treats ready.
4. Present the object to the dog by either putting it on the floor or by holding it in your hand.

5. Click and feed your dog for looking at it.

6. Click and feed your dog for approaching it.

7. Click and feed your dog for touching it with his mouth only.

8. Click and feed your dog for any kind of mouth movement on the object. If it looks like your dog has no intention of putting his mouth on it, put a treat on top of the object and, when the dog goes to eat it, click as the dog opens his mouth. Give your dog another treat.

9. Click and feed your dog for picking up the object.

10. Once your dog is actually picking up the object, start to lengthen the amount of time, by a second or two at a time, that the dog has the object in his mouth by withholding the click.

11. Begin to generalize this behavior to other quiet areas. Repeat Steps 5 to 10.

12. Continue to lengthen the time that your dog has the item in his mouth.

13. When your dog can hold the object for one minute, start changing your dog's body position. Teach him to hold the object in a sit, stand, down, and while heeling.

Secrets of success:

• Make sure to click as the dog is holding the object, not as he's letting it go.

• Teach the dog to hold many different objects, ones that vary in size, shape, and texture.

• If, in the future, you are going to teach your dog to retrieve, make sure to teach your dog how to hold the object first.

• Slowly increase the amount of time for which your dog can hold the object. Asking too much too quickly will weaken the behavior.

Emergency Recall Cue

The emergency recall cue is a powerful cue to use only in an emergency and only after your standard recall cue has failed.

Especially helpful when...

- Your small dog slips out the front door of your apartment complex, which is currently undergoing construction. Once outside, he is frightened by all the loud noises. Blindly, he runs straight into the path of a bulldozer that is backing up. You scream and tell him to come. He does not respond. Praying to yourself, you yell your emergency recall cue. Because of the highly variable reinforcing properties that this cue represents, he spins around and starts running toward you. Now you call him to come to you and he comes readily.

- Your dog begins to explode at another dog. In order to cut through the explosion midstream, you say your dog's emergency recall cue. Startled, he looks up at you as if to say, "What?" You reward him and ask for an alternative behavior.

How to make it happen:

1. Choose the word that you will condition. When choosing an emergency recall word:
   - Make sure it is a word that will easily come to mind in an emergency situation.
   - Refrain from using a word that your dog commonly hears, such as his name or the cue that you would normally use to ask your dog to come to you.

2. Once you have chosen your word, choose a highly delectable treat that your dog will get only when this particular word is spoken.

3. For the next two to three weeks, simply say the word and give your dog one of these precious treats. Remember that, at this point, your dog does not have to perform any particular kind of behavior to get this reward. You are simply teaching your dog to associate the sound of this word with the reward, just as you might teach him to associate the sound of the clicker with a reward.

4. Practice Step 3, seven to ten times per day, variably and unpredictably throughout the course of the day.

5. Test the cue once after a week.

6. Go into another room.

7. Wait until your dog is busy doing another activity.

8. Say the word loudly and watch how quickly your dog flies to you.

9. Reward the behavior.

10. As your dog grows to love this word, feel free to vary the reinforcers that you are using.

11. For maintenance, keep the word primed by conditioning three to five times each day.

Secrets of success:

• Be careful not to overuse this emergency cue. This cue is only to be used in a situation when your conventional recall cue has failed.

• At the start of each day, put seven to ten treats in your pocket. Make sure that your pocket is empty before you go to bed at night.

• Remember, you are only creating a positive association between the word your dog hears with the wonderful treat that he is getting. Do not ask the dog for a particular behavior before you give him his treat. Simply say the word and reward him.

• Initially your dog is never to hear this word unless it is followed by a treat.

Name Recognition

When you've taught your dog to recognize his name, he gives you his attention whenever you call his name, regardless of environment or circumstances.

Especially helpful when…

• Your dog begins to be aggressive toward another dog. You say his name, and he stops and looks up as if to say, "What?" You have squelched the episode and prepared your dog for further instructions.

- Your dog is playing at the park and another dog growls at a third. Concerned that your dog will join in, you call his name. He turns his attention to you and returns to your side.
- Your dog is about to jump on a visitor. You say your dog's name. He stops and looks at you for further instruction.

How to make it happen:

1. Say your dog's name. Click and feed your dog. Do not ask your dog to perform a specific behavior. His name means a click and a treat, as simple as that.
2. Repeat the above procedure in varied environments.
3. If you have multiple dogs living in the same household, work this behavior with each dog separately.
4. Refrain from using your dog's name in casual conversation. If this is impossible, choose a specific name (close to the original name, e.g., Nick is now Nicholas) by which you can signal your dog.

Secrets of success:

- Always reinforce your dog for looking at you voluntarily, especially when you say his name.
- Say your dog's name before you give him an instruction. For example, before you ask your dog to come to you, say your dog's name so that you will have his full attention and then give the next cue. Click and treat for compliance.
- Never use your dog's name to scold or punish him.

Creativity

The foundation behaviors presented in this chapter provide a collection of ways to communicate with your dog. Teach these behaviors, and you will always have a way to tell your dog to stay with you, to walk with you, or to come to you when you call him. The ability to communicate these messages is important for any handler, but especially for those working with a fearful or aggressive dog.

These training exercises are also an ideal way to keep your dog's mind stimulated every day. Your dog is a thinking being. He learns something every minute of every day. The important question is, "What is he learning?" Without some guidance from you, he will create his own curriculum, which may not be the one you have in mind.

Dogs, like humans, should be given the opportunity to use their minds freely, without the threat of punishment. Teaching your dog to experiment with his own behavior is not only fun and exciting for your dog, but it is also a very important piece of his rehabilitation into a calm, safe animal. It helps him to build confidence in his decision-making abilities. Just as writing or painting can be a form of therapy for a human, teaching your dog to invent behavior, what clicker trainers call "free shaping," can be therapeutic for your dog. This exercise is "freeing," especially for dogs with an inhibited or abusive background.

Try this free shaping exercise: You would like to teach your dog to push an object with his nose. Begin free shaping this behavior by putting a cardboard box on the floor and doing nothing until your dog does something—anything—with the box. Click and feed him if he looks at it, sniffs it, paws it, steps into it, and so on. Let your dog experiment with the box. You may be amazed at his creativity. Because you've decided that you would like him to learn to push with his nose, you click when he touches the box with his nose. Once he is doing that consistently, then change your criteria for earning a click:

He must now shove the box with his nose. Once that is happening repeatedly, save your click until he moves the box several inches with a shove of his nose, and so on. Or follow the same steps to teach your dog to sit in the box, or push it with his paw, or anything else you can think of or that your dog suggests with his experimentation.

Free shaping is the process of letting the dog develop a behavior by offering, in the beginning, random behaviors. The trainer then captures and reinforces small, successful approximations of a desired behavior, eventually shaping them toward a finished behavior. The dog seeks information provided by the clicks to build the correct behavior gradually. Dogs whose behaviors have been trained through free shaping show amazing creativity. They have learned initiative and, as a result, sense some control over their environment. They find their environments, therefore, less threatening. Free shaping will also help you improve your timing and teach you to observe the smallest movements of your dog, as well as to think on the spur of the moment. These skills will be extremely helpful as you bring your dog into stressful environments and settings.

From Jitters to Joy: The Emotional Switch

Clicker training games, such as free shaping, can change your worried, stressed dog into a playful, joyful companion. Once you are both clicker-savvy and clicker-creative, teach your dog a movement or a game that he really enjoys and put it on a verbal cue or a hand cue. For example, I taught my dog Ben to jump straight up and touch his nose to the palm of my hand if I said "Where's the monster?" Anytime that I could see his spirits sinking, I would give him his cue to jump, and it was as if someone had tickled him. He would jump straight up with tail wagging and mouth grinning. His whole demeanor changed from one of tension and stress to one of exuberance and joy. His body posture immediately softened. He thought this was a great game. It brought him instant relaxation.

Experiment with different behaviors and see which activity your dog enjoys the most. You can build them the same way you build your foundation behaviors. Put a cue on the behavior and call it up anytime your dog needs an emotional alteration. Here are a few examples:

- Targeting to hand
- Jump up
- Tug-of-war
- Spin
- Play bow
- Give paw
- Weave through legs

Engaging in playful activities can lift the emotions of any animal. Change your dog's behavior first and the attitude will follow. Have fun with your training, and your dog will begin to relax and have fun too.

CHAPTER 3

The Process of Clicking with an Aggressive Dog

Aggressive behavior can be sculpted like any other behavior. The only difference is that, in treating aggression, we need to *lower* the frequency of the aggressive behavior and *increase* the frequency of the appropriate incompatible behaviors that we have previously taught our dogs. Just as we can use the clicker to strengthen the frequency of a behavior, we can also use the clicker to lessen the frequency, and intensity, of a behavior. We can click a behavior into extinction by gradually shaping its absence, which is why clicker training is so powerful for treating aggression.

The first lesson that your dog needs to learn is that he can exist peacefully in the chaotic environment that he finds so aversive, whether it be a veterinarian's office or a dog training class. I call this clicking for the "state of being," reinforcing the dog for simply *existing* in the difficult environment. The exercises that follow will teach your dog to relax and focus on you, his trusted handler, in response to stimuli that in the past have invoked feelings of fear or panic. He needs to be able to relax and focus so that you can ask him to perform more appropriate, incompatible behaviors. To do so, he needs to be desensitized to aversive stimuli.

Desensitization training is a form of counterconditioning that reduces an inappropriate response to an event. The process involves first working with the dog at the lowest levels of arousal and then gradually increasing the distractions as success is achieved at each level. We can begin this process by clicking and feeding the dog at the lowest points of intensity of the aggressive behavior, or if your dog is not that highly reactive, in the *absence* of the behavior that we would like to see disappear. Having the ability to mark the behavior at its lowest points will not only cause an overall decline in the intensity of the aggressive behavior, but it will also create tiny, ever-widening windows of calm behavior, which will make it easier for you to mark the correct behavior repeatedly.

In order for you to be able to reinforce those lowest points of intensity, you must be able to accurately read your dog's body language, and to recognize the earliest signs of stress in your dog. Stress signals can include the following: dilated pupils, increased respiration and heart rate, shallow or rapid breathing, any kind of vocalization, mounting, excessive shedding, hard ridges around the eyes and mouth, stiff body, freezing, trying to run away, not interested in food, glazed eyes or "whale" eye (showing the whites of his eyes), and any kind of behavior that you would consider unusual for your dog.

Being able to read your dog's stress signals is vital in preventing an aggressive explosion. The more agitated your dog becomes, the higher the risk that your dog will start exhibiting aggressive behavior. Lunging, barking, growling, snapping, foaming at the mouth, raised hackles, staring eyes, and baring teeth are all common signs that your dog has become overly aroused. The risk of your dog biting, at this stage, has greatly increased.

The following training recipes offer ways in which you can step in and reinforce the absence of stress before it develops into reactive, aggressive displays. You will then be able to fill those openings in your dog's behavior with positive, alternative behaviors.

If your dog gets extremely agitated when he sees another dog from any distance you should begin with "Extinguishing Cues to Aggression in Highly Reactive Dogs" (see page 74). Your goal is to make "dents" of silence and calm in the noisy and chaotic behavior in which your over-reactive dog indulges when he is frightened. These first steps are often the most difficult to take. Once you have begun, progress will come more quickly.

The second recipe, "Clicking for the Absence of the Aggressive Behavior," will teach you how to continue to reinforce calm behavior as well as how to use reinforcement to create a "thinking" dog that can perform behaviors that are incompatible with aggression.

The third recipe in this chapter, "Selective Reactivity," is for dogs that just can't stand certain individual dogs. It doesn't matter why your dog doesn't like another dog; you just want to teach him to tolerate its presence, and this recipe will show you how.

Once you have worked through these training recipes, your dog will play an active role in keeping himself safe. Before accomplishing this, your dog was a victim of his own environment and, possibly, his distraught owner. With patience, consistency, and clicker training, you can give your dog techniques to control his environment through the decisions he makes; looking to you for guidance is one such technique that will help in stressful situations. Empowered with alternative solutions, your dog will gain confidence and stay calm in trying circumstances.

Why Punishment Does Not Work

Aggressive behavior is challenging to modify, in part because it usually evokes an emotional response in the handler. Though aggression is a perfectly normal canine behavior, it frightens and embarrasses humans. It even feels like a personal insult to handlers who take pride in having taken excellent care of their dog. Aggressive behavior is wrenching to us: we know a biting dog is unacceptable, but this dog is our dog and we feel compelled to save him. Our responsibility for our animals' lives never feels quite so acute as when faced with chronic aggression.

It is no wonder, then, that we seek methods that seem to guarantee quick fixes. Physical punishment seems an obvious answer. If a dog "goes off" at another dog, hang him on a prong collar or zap him with an electronic collar. If the consequence is sufficiently severe and immediate, shouldn't it wipe the behavior out of the dog's brain? First of all, punishment is bad because it's abusive. Second, it may be effective in that it halts the behavior as it is happening, yet over time the frequency and intensity of the punishment needs to be increased to maintain the original threshold of suppressed behavior. The dog becomes at risk from the implementation of the punishment itself, as well as the disastrous side effects that commonly occur, including hypervigilance, irrational fear, heightened irritability, impulsive/explosive behavior, hyperactivity, aggression evoked with minimal provocation, withdrawal and social avoidance, loss of sensitivity to pleasure and pain, and depressed mood.

In the case of my dog Ben, the side effects of the punishment were more difficult to deal with than the original behavior it was meant to cure. He soon reacted viciously to all dogs, rather than growling at just a few. He became afraid of environments in which he formerly felt comfortable. He was leery of garbage cans, sheets blowing in the wind, and stop signs.

Punishment can damage the relationships we have with our dogs. You want your dog to feel safe near you, not threatened. Fear stops the learning process in both dogs and humans. If the threat comes from the source of learning (the handler), the decrease in learning is compounded.

The most serious danger with punishment, however, is that it very often feels good to the punisher. Punishment is reinforcing to the punisher. It mistakenly leads us to believe that we have "fixed" the behavior. The next time we will be tempted to punish harder and faster.

Not only is punishment risky, but it also fails to teach the dog an acceptable alternate behavior. The dog does not *learn* what to do the next time he is in that same situation. He only learns to fear the situation. To adequately solve the aggressive behavior, you need to ask yourself, "What do I want my dog to do, other than being aggressive, when he sees another dog?"

Training Recipes: Reducing Aggression

Extinguishing Cues to Aggression in Highly Reactive Dogs

When your dog is under stress, he may be unable to perform trained behaviors. If he is reacting intensely to the stressor, he may not even hear your cues. You can, however, teach your dog to be calm in environments that he usually finds aversive. I call this "clicking for a peaceful state of mind." Your dog needs to be able to remain calm in a stressful situation *before* he has the ability to make choices while under stress. And he needs to learn this before you can ask him to perform known alternative behaviors.

While these exercises are for dogs that are highly reactive to the presence of another dog in the environment, they are appropriate for any dog that is highly sensitive to any stimulus.

Especially helpful when…

- Your dog cannot perform any behavior that you ask, because of stress produced by his immediate environment.

How to make it happen:

1. Put your dog in his head collar with a six-foot lead attached. Consider using a muzzle if necessary.

2. Get your clicker and have a plentiful supply of tasty treats easily accessible in a pouch. Use extra-special treats that your dog is given only when you are working on this specific behavior.

3. Figure out beforehand which hand you will hold your clicker in, which hand you will hold the leash in, and how you will quickly feed the dog after you click. Make sure you feel comfortable clicking and feeding your dog, at a high rate of reinforcement, while still controlling your dog on the leash.

4. Work in an environment where there will be safe access to whatever your dog

finds aversive (the sight of another dog, for example). Make sure the setup is such that you can adjust your distance to the other dog easily. In this way you can establish a threshold in which to expose your dog in successful degrees. The threshold is the distance from which your dog can withstand the sight of another dog without showing any aggressive behavior. Think of it as your dog's comfort zone. Be sure to choose an environment where other dogs will not run up to yours off-leash accidentally.

5. Have a friend, with her stable, nonreactive dog, meet you at a park or wooded area. Make sure she keeps her dog on-leash. Walk the perimeter of an area from which your dog will be able to see your friend's dog at a distance. Expose your dog to the other dog at the distance you feel marks his threshold. It may be ten feet away, it may be fifty. If your dog displays aggressive behavior, widen the space until you find the point at which your dog can remain calm. Then expose your dog for a very short period of time to your friend's dog, perhaps thirty seconds.

6. Move your dog toward the other dog until he begins to behave aggressively. Click and feed him at the lowest points of intensity of the aggressive behavior. By marking the behavior at its lowest points you will not only cause an overall decline in the intensity of the aggression, but it will also create small windows of calm behavior, which will make it easier for you to mark the correct behavior repeatedly. The more calm behavior you can click, the calmer your dog will be.

7. If you do not see even the smallest lessening of intensity in the aggressive display, click and treat your dog each time he takes a breath. Click and feed for a second of quiet in between aggressive behavior.

    •   Be sure to wear gloves if your dog takes treats forcefully. As he begins to calm down, this behavior will disappear.

    •   Do not be surprised if your dog does not eat after you click. Click and give your dog the treat. If he does not want it, let it drop to the ground. Whether or not your dog feels comfortable eating can be an indicator of his stress or comfort level. If he does not eat, simply clean up the treats when your training session is done. As your dog calms down and as behavior improves, he will begin to eat the treats.

8. Work on one aspect of your dog's behavior at a time. As your dog becomes more successful, slowly lengthen the time for which he is exposed to the other dog. Then slowly decrease the space between the dogs. Keep the session short.

9. As your dog continues to improve, either expose your dog to more dogs in the environment or ask your dog to perform a simple behavior in the presence of the other dog. For best results, work both of these pieces simultaneously, as your dog becomes more experienced.

10. As your dog progresses, proceed to the next recipe, "Clicking for the Absence of the Aggressive Behavior."

Secrets of success:

- Plan each session.
- Ignore the temptation to overexpose your dog when he's being successful.
- Click and feed your dog quickly and repeatedly as you begin to expose him to other dog(s). Use soft, highly palatable treats. Practice the speed of delivery at home first before going on location.
- Feed your dog his meal after the training session for that day. Take into account how much he has eaten during the training session and adjust his daily meal accordingly to prevent weight gain.
- Exercise your dog before training sessions, if possible.
- Try to expose your dog only to calm dogs that will ignore his tirade rather than respond to it with one of their own.
- Record the day your dog begins to eat in the training session; it marks a significant breakthrough.

Clicking for the Absence of the Aggressive Behavior

If your dog has begun to behave more calmly in the presence of other dogs, you are ready to click and feed *before* he reacts to them. Your goal is to increase the time that your dog can tolerate stress before he displays aggression. Now that your dog can "think" despite the presence of a stressful stimulus, you will be able to train him to perform alternative foundation behaviors such as eye contact.

Especially helpful when…

- You want your dog to look at you instead of reacting to another dog or person.

How to make it happen:

1. Review Steps 1 to 5 in the previous recipe, "Extinguishing Cues to Aggression in Highly Reactive Dogs."
2. Work in short successful sessions. (Remember, the brain learns habitual behavior in small pieces.)
3. Click and feed your dog for looking at another dog.
4. Click and feed your dog for listening to another dog in the environment, for example when other dogs pant, bark, whine, growl, and so on.
5. Click and feed your dog for allowing another dog to look at him.
6. Click and feed your dog if another dog moves his body toward him in any way.
7. Click and feed your dog if he happens to glance up at you.
8. Click and feed your dog for any type of self-calming behavior that he might display, for example turning his head away from the other dog, turning his body away, yawning, and so forth (see page 120).
9. Click and feed for any appropriate response that the reactive dog offers that is not aggressive in nature.

    (By practicing Steps 3 through 9, your dog, in anticipation of the click and treat, will start looking at you. Soon the presence of the other dog in the environment will automatically become the cue to look at you. In this way, you do not have to manually try to get your dog's attention every time another dog enters the area.)

10. Click and feed your dog for looking at another dog, then sitting and looking up at you.

11. If your dog explodes at any time, it means you went too far, too fast. Work within your successful threshold level and slowly lengthen the exposure. To shorten the duration of the explosion:

   • Use your emergency cue (see page 62). Click and feed when the aggressive behavior is interrupted.

   • Begin walking backward and tell your dog to sit and ask for eye contact. (See page 40 for Sit, and page 38 for Eye Contact.) Your dog, because of the backward motion of your body, should fall into "Front" position. Click and feed for his full attention on you.

   • Pivot 180 degrees with your dog at your left side so now both of you have your backs to the distractions in the environment. Click and feed your dog for staying by your side while you've pivoted.

12. As your dog continues to get used to the presence of other dogs, take him for walks with another dog-and-handler team. Make sure the other dog is a stable, nonreactive dog. Click and feed all appropriate nonaggressive behavior.

   • Visit a few environments full of potential encounters and obstacles for your dog: parking lots, wooded areas, places where there are likely to be on-leash dogs. Heel in and around the obstacles so that the dogs do not focus solely on each other.

   • Walk forward in parallel lines with your partner dog-and-handler team. Then cross each other in opposite directions.

Secrets of success:

Leave the environment only when your dog is calm and cooperative. If you were to discontinue the session every time your dog reacted aggressively, your session would grow shorter and shorter. Your dog really does not want to be there; leaving the environment, therefore, is a reward in itself. You need to teach your dog that acceptable behavior is the only thing that will earn him the right to leave the area and end the training session.

Selective Reactivity

This training recipe will help if your dog gets along with most dogs but is consistently aggressive toward certain individual dogs or particular sorts of dogs.

Especially helpful when…

- Your dog likes every dog except the one who lives right next door, or belongs to your new spouse, or … well, you get the idea.

How to make it happen:

1. Identify the "problem" dog, and discuss your training plan and goal with the dog's owner. If your dog is aggressive toward a certain breed or kind of dog, find a cooperative owner of an individual within that breed and discuss your goal.
2. Review the previous training recipes for "Extinguishing Cues to Aggression in Highly Reactive Dogs" and "Clicking for the Absence of the Aggressive Behavior." Depending on the severity of your dog's reactivity, start with the most appropriate training protocol.
3. Work in small steps, advancing with successful achievement.
4. Supervise all interactions between your dog and the "problem" dog.

5. Plan a time for both dogs and handlers to go for a walk together, initially with both dogs on leash. Keep the walk as relaxed as possible, with the dogs at a distance that makes this possible.

6. In another session, clicker train both dogs in the same room with each owner handling her own dog, and each dog on leash. In this way, the dogs can share a working environment.

7. Have the dogs take a group obedience or agility class together.

8. Create a team-based behavior in which both dogs can work with their handlers simultaneously. The dogs will need to work together cooperatively in order to receive reinforcement. Here are a few examples:

    • One dog is being taught a behavior, such as holding an object, while the other dog sits and watches. When one dog is clicked and fed for learning the behavior, the other is rewarded for waiting patiently. Alternate roles.

    • One dog does a sit/stay while the other performs a down/stay or stand/stay.

    • One dog performs a behavior while sitting on a chair or table, and the other dog performs a different behavior underneath the chair or table.

9. As the dogs become more comfortable with each other, let them engage in more and more fun behaviors.

10. Go slowly when allowing the dogs off-leash. Let the nonreactive dog off the leash first and, if all goes well, allow the other dog off the leash. (Only do this if it is safe to do so. Make sure to muzzle the problem dog if you are not sure how he will react.)

11. If possible, let the dogs interact for a short period of time. Do not let them get overstimulated.

12. Slowly allow the dogs more and more interaction. If at any time the dogs misbehave, end the session and put both dogs in a "time-out."

Secrets of success:

- Let the dogs slowly become accustomed to seeing each other.

- Never leave both dogs alone to fight it out.

- Only allow the dogs to do "busy" activities in which they can focus on the activity itself rather than on each other.

- Feed the dogs lots of treats when they are in each other's presence. Make sure that each handler feeds his or her own dog to avoid competition over a food source.

What About *Your* Behavior?

This book may be about training your dog, but *your* behavior is an important part of the puzzle and must be addressed as well. Your dog's aggressive tendencies may not be a result of anything you've done; nevertheless, they're bound to produce a behavioral response in you. Rarely are handlers advised to pay attention to their own emotional responses and expressions of fear. This is unfortunate because your own fear and stress may be your dog's first and clearest cue that something in the environment is terribly wrong; picking up those signals from you puts the dog in aggressive mode.

Dogs are acute readers of body language, both human and canine, and handlers of aggressive dogs must try to reduce their signs of stress whenever they are with their dogs. What do you do, though, if it is simply impossible to relax fully? What if you cannot control your body language, if you cannot prevent the sudden intake of breath, the tense hand on the leash, the grab of the collar? After all, as handlers, we too have been punished by our dogs' explosions of aggression. The consequences of that punishment are as uncontrollable as those of any other punishment.

While we do need to learn to control our responses as much as possible, much of our body language is involuntary. No matter how much we reduce our body language, our dogs are so finely attuned to it that they will still pick up some signals. But what would happen if we were to change the meaning of the words and phrases in our body language? What if, whether it is a suddenly tight leash or a hand on the muzzle, our own signs of stress were to become specific behavior cues to our dogs? Just as we can clicker train any behavior, we can change the meaning of any cue. Thus we can change what our stress reactions mean to our dogs, from a cue for fear to a cue for calm.

I suspected while working with Ben that he was responding to my body language as much as he was to the sight of another dog. So I conducted a little experiment. I took him out into the yard where there were no other dogs around. We walked, on-leash, as we normally would. Suddenly, as if I had seen another dog approaching, I sucked in my breath and tightened the leash. Ben immediately became aggressive; he also moved his head back and forth scanning the perimeters of the yard. He was convinced that there was another dog in the immediate area. My body language and tight leash were his cue to be aggressive, as much or more so than the sight of another dog.

Because I feared my stress might be impossible to erase completely if we were actually faced with another dog, I needed to change Ben's response to my behavior, to teach him that a tight leash is his cue to make eye contact with me—quickly! Once we had eye contact, I could ask him to perform a behavior incompatible with aggression.

The process of changing our stress cues to cues for behavior is in part desensitization—getting our dogs used to the handling we do under stress. It also requires operant conditioning, or teaching new behaviors in response to cues. You can teach your dog to move into the leash when he feels it pulled tight, to turn and look at you when you sharply draw in your breath, and to love to have your hands on his muzzle and collar.

The process also requires you to become acutely aware of your physical responses to stress. When you've identified the elements of your own physical behavior, and begun using them in training as cues for your dog's behavior, you too can begin to practice self-control in tense situations. If your dog is taught to remain calm while you are exhibiting stress cues, then encounters that were previously punishing to you will become positively reinforcing, and your stress behavior will lessen in intensity.

Keeping a Training Journal

The first step to modifying your own behavior is to keep a training journal. No matter what your training goal, a journal will help you plan your training sessions and track your progress. When training an aggressive dog, a training journal gives you a place to reflect on your own emotions and behavior. Writing down your responses to your dog's aggressive displays, and to his better moments, will help you recognize the behaviors you display under stress, as well as giving you an outlet to relieve that stress. Keeping a journal will soon become self-reinforcing: you can review the entries you've made over time and see how far you've come.

I suggest purchasing a two-subject notebook. Dedicate the first half to your dog's behavior, and the second half to your reflections and your behavior. In the first half of your journal, date each entry and label it with the behavior you are working on. Jot down the time you started and the time you ended. Record the starting level of the behavior and the ending level. You are collecting data, so keep the information as plain as possible.

Then, after each training session—especially after a major breakthrough or a distressing explosion—record what you felt during and after the session in the second half of your journal. Are you elated because your dog finally began to eat treats while in the presence of another dog? Are you discouraged because your dog, who has not exploded in months, suddenly lost it? Did you lose it, and punish your dog? What was the impact on his behavior? Write it all down. Empty it on to the page so that you may enter your next training session free of any baggage from the last one. You want to begin each session without an expectation of failure and without a false sense of security.

With consistent record keeping, the behaviors you have reinforced and the change in your dog's behavior—the reinforcement history—is there for you to examine whenever you need to find answers to your training questions. You may forget how far your dog has come in the face of inevitable, occasional setbacks. Your training journal will enable you to assess the situation objectively and plan your next step.

If you aren't certain how to assess and plan training sessions, use your training journal to help you learn to observe your dog. Your dog will teach you what you need to know. Write down your observations of his behavior, and they will become sharper. Study his behavior, and you will be able to decide how you want to modify it. Record each success, as well as your challenges and setbacks, so that you have the strength to move forward.

Know your goal for each training session, and plan the steps that will get you there. (The recipes in this book are designed to help you develop this approach for any behavior.) Follow your training plan, and adjust it in subsequent sessions according to your observations. Collect the data so that you can assess your progress objectively, rather than through memory molded by emotion.

Changing Stress Cues to Calm Cues

Observe, identify, and list your stress cues in your training journal. What physical signs do you exhibit when you fear your dog is about to show aggression? You may want to ask a friend to videotape you as you walk with your dog in a potentially threatening environment. Review the tape and write down what you see. For example: "When I see another dog walking toward us, I cross the street with my dog," "I pull up on the leash, and drag my dog away," "I change the tone of voice in which I talk to my dog." These are your signs of stress. For your dog, they may be cues to be aggressive as much as is the sight of another dog.

Work with each stress cue separately. To change the meaning of each event, perform the stress signal in the company of your dog, at a very low intensity, and click and feed your dog as it is happening. If your voice changes when you are stressed, put your dog on-leash and mimic what you might say to an approaching stranger. Say it softly first. Click and treat your dog as you say it. Now raise the tone of your voice. Click and feed your dog. Gradually increase the volume of your words. Click and feed your dog.

By clicking and feeding your dog each time you speak in your stressed voice, you are teaching him that this change in your voice equals a click and a treat. With persistence and consistency, instead of lunging at the end of the leash or cowering when he hears you raise your voice, your dog simply looks at you for a click and treat. He remains calm and in control.

The following training recipes focus on four common behaviors that handlers exhibit when faced with an aggressive display: tightening the leash, grabbing the collar, holding the dog's mouth shut, and moving quickly in the opposite direction. Each may cue a dog to react aggressively. If you have identified other behaviors of your own that may have become signals for your dog to show aggression, the principles remain the same. By clicking and feeding your dog while you exhibit your stress signals, you will change his associated behavior.

Training Recipes: Changing Stress Cues to Calm Cues

Tightening the Leash

Once you've worked on this recipe with your dog, he will read your leash-tightening reaction as a cue to look at you calmly and await further instructions, rather than a cue to prepare for an aggressive encounter with another dog.

Especially helpful when...

- Your dog meets other dogs. As your dog begins to sniff the other dog, you tense up and the leash goes tight. Follow the steps in this recipe, and instead of exploding, your dog will turn away from the other dog, give you eye contact, and loosen the leash himself. You can now ask for another behavior or simply move on.

How to make it happen:

1. Let your dog go to the end of the leash.
2. Take a step back.
3. Click and feed your dog the moment the leash goes taut.
4. Allow the dog to come to you to get the treat.
5. Repeat several times.
6. Once you've mastered Steps 1 to 5, stay in one spot and pull up on the leash.
7. Click and feed your dog for loosening the leash by coming toward you.
8. Gradually increase the amount of pressure with which you pull the leash tight.
9. Alternate between standing still and taking a step back.
10. As you continue to work this behavior, also reinforce any eye contact that occurs. At the sensation of his leash tightening, your dog, anticipating the click and treat, will move closer to you to loosen the leash; looking at you should become a natural part of this process.

11. When your dog consistently turns toward you when you pull up tightly on the leash, take your training sessions into a variety of distracting environments. Doing so will build up your confidence as well as your dog's.

Secrets of success:

- Tighten the leash very gradually so that the pressure on your dog's collar is very slight at first; looking at you in response to this slight pressure should earn him a click and a treat. Increase the pressure in tiny increments.
- If at any time your dog seems nervous, stop the exercise and go back to the previous level of success.

Touching/Grabbing Your Dog's Collar

When dog handlers get tense, a common reaction is to reach down and grab the dog by the collar. Dogs are dragged into their crates, out of training buildings, and into the veterinarian's office. Because of the handler's anxiety in the heat of the moment, the dragging is often done roughly and harshly. It is no surprise then that dogs learn to shy away from human hands, especially as they reach toward the dog's face or neck. Ideally, your dog will respond to a cue to move into his crate or out of a potentially explosive situation. But if not, and you or someone else should grab his collar, you want the dog's response to be calm acceptance, even a lick and a wag, rather than a growl or a bite.

Especially helpful when…

- Visitors have just arrived, your dog is not responding to his "Kennel up" cue, and you need him in his crate immediately.
- At the veterinarian's office, the vet tech moves your dog from the scale to the exam table by yanking on his collar.

- Your dog runs into the street and a neighbor, concerned for your dog's safety, grabs him by the collar.

How to make it happen:

1. Touch your dog's neck lightly.
2. Click and feed your dog while your fingers are still on his neck.
3. Touch your dog's neck with a little more pressure.
4. Click and feed your dog for happily accepting the touch.
5. Touch your dog's collar with a couple of fingers.
6. Click and feed your dog for acceptance.
7. Touch your dog's collar with three fingers, four, then five.
8. Click and feed your dog for tolerance.
9. Now take one finger and loop it around the collar.
10. Click and feed for compliance.
11. Build up to having all your fingers looped into the collar.
12. Click and feed for patient cooperation.

Now that your dog is allowing you to take a hold of his collar without incident:

1. Change your body position while holding the collar.
2. Click and treat your dog for allowing you to:
   - Sit, while holding him by the collar.
   - Stand, while holding him by the collar.
   - Walk slowly, while holding him by the collar.
3. Take one step with your hand on the collar.
4. Click and feed.
5. Take two steps and so on. Click and feed for all compliant behavior.
6. Build up the speed at which you are escorting him. Remember, at this point, you are not dragging the dog by the collar but merely guiding him.

As your dog becomes comfortable with you leading him by his collar, isolate the act of exerting pressure on the collar separately:

1. Ask your dog to sit.
2. Pull up gently on his collar.
3. Click and feed your dog as you pull up gently.
4. Gradually increase the amount of pressure on the collar. (Always practice this exercise in a controlled manner.)
5. Once the dog is comfortable with the amount of pressure on the collar, then increase the speed at which you take the collar. Eventually you should be able to take the dog by the collar without the dog considering it a threat.

Now that your dog will let you exert more pressure on his collar, combine the two pieces of the behavior:

1. Click and feed your dog as you walk him by the collar pulling gently.
2. Click and feed your dog as you begin to pull him by the collar.

As your dog becomes more comfortable with this behavior, practice it in a number of new environments. Have family and friends start from square one and work on this exercise with your dog. Remember: safety always comes first! If your dog at any time seems afraid or uncertain, end the exercise. You may have asked for too much, too soon. Drop back to where your dog was successful and work from there.

Secrets of success:

- Make sure to use a buckle collar to work this exercise. Never use a choke collar.
- Do not allow anyone else to drag your dog by his collar while the behavior is still in the process of being trained.
- Increase the pressure on the collar gradually as your dog becomes used to it.

Walking with Your Hand on Your Dog's Muzzle (Chin Targeting)

It is not uncommon to see handlers at dog shows or competitions weaving their way through crowds of dogs and people with a hand encircling their dog's muzzle. The handler's palm supports the dog's chin and his or her thumb rests on top of the muzzle. Having the ability to walk your dog in this fashion can make you feel more secure if you find yourself in a chaotic, stressful environment. If your dog is not comfortable with this type of handling, you risk a bite.

Especially helpful when…

- You are at an obedience class and you come head-to-head with another dog and his owner in a doorway. You quickly encircle your dog's muzzle and walk safely through.

- You are at your veterinarian's office. To reach the exam room, you must pass by several owners with their dogs sniffing at the end of their leash. You're concerned about the close quarters in which you and your dog must maneuver, but you step out briskly, encircling your dog's muzzle with your hand as you go.

How to make it happen:

Before you begin this exercise, consider which side you walk your dog on. This is the hand that will encircle the dog's muzzle as you walk. If you walk your dog on the left, escort him with your left hand while your right hand holds the leash.

1. Touch the top of your dog's nose.
2. Click and feed your dog.
3. Repeat several times.
4. Cup your hand under your dog's chin.
5. Click and feed your dog.
6. Repeat several times.
7. Now alternate between the two behaviors (Steps 1 and 4).

8. Next, cup your dog's chin in the palm of your hand and let your fingers ride up on one side of his mouth. Allow your thumb to rest lightly on top of the dog's muzzle.

9. Click and feed for compliance.

10. Cup your dog's chin in the palm of your hand and let your fingers ride up on the other side of his mouth.

11. Click and feed.

12. Now alternate Steps 8 and 10.

13. Continue working until your dog is comfortable with you cupping your hand underneath his chin and extending your fingers up so that your hand encompasses his entire muzzle on both sides.

Now that your dog allows you to take hold of his muzzle, change your body position while holding his muzzle.

1. Click and treat your dog for allowing you to:
    *   Sit, while holding his chin on the palm of your hand.
    *   Stand, while holding his chin on the palm of your hand.
    *   Walk slowly, while letting his chin sit on the palm of your hand.

2. Take one step while supporting the dog's chin. Click and feed.

3. Take two steps while supporting the dog's chin. Continue to click and feed for compliance.

4. As the dog allows you to gently support his chin, add the rest of your fingers on each side of his face. Repeat the previous steps until your dog is totally calm.

5. Increase your walking speed while you have your hand on his muzzle. At this point, do not grab your dog by the muzzle and hold tightly. You are merely supporting his chin with your fingers.

6. When your dog is comfortable with you holding his muzzle as you walk a few

paces, attach a leash to your dog's collar (or Gentle Leader) and practice the maneuver in settings that more closely approximate realistic situations.

7. Practice the behavior in increasingly distracting and stressful environments.

Secrets of success:

*   Proceed slowly and never quickly grab at your dog's face.
*   Rest your thumb lightly on top of the dog's nose as the rest of your hand and fingers support the dog's chin.
*   Never use this gesture as a means of punishment or intimidation.
*   Build up duration and distraction level separately.

Turning and Moving in the Opposite Direction

You should always have the option of simply turning away from whatever frightens your dog. He should follow you calmly in the opposite direction, whether you are walking slowly or moving swiftly away from a potentially dangerous situation. The behavior can even become one of your dog's favorite games. He will read your sudden decision to reverse course—a handler stress cue—as a game you like to play.

Especially helpful when…

*   You're walking your dog down a narrow sidewalk. Another person comes toward you with her dog on the same side of the street. To avoid a confrontation, you decide to cross quickly to the opposite side of the street and continue on your way, or you turn around and walk in the opposite direction.
*   You are in a pet store picking up dog food. As you proceed down one of the aisles, two of the other customers' dogs begin to fight. You tell your dog, "Let's go," turn in the opposite direction, and proceed down another aisle. Your dog happily complies instead of jumping into the fray.

How to make it happen:

1. Work with your dog in a distraction-free setting.

2. Attach a leash to your dog's collar.

3. Walk forward with your dog at your side, as you would normally.

4. Do an "about-face" turn (pivot 180 degrees) and move in the opposite direction.

5. Click and feed your dog just as he concludes the pivot.

6. Repeat several times.

7. Now increase the speed at which you turn.

8. Click and feed your dog for quickly turning with you.

9. Repeat several times.

10. As your dog begins to learn this behavior, assign a verbal cue to the physical act of turning away. You might choose a word or phrase that will come naturally to you in stressful situations: "Whoops" or "Outta here!" Or, consider the cues you already display to your dog when you are in a tense situation. Do you hold your breath? Gasp? Or say "Oh, no?" Let one of those signals become your cue for a sudden change of direction.

11. Walk with your dog, say your selected cue, and run in the opposite direction. Click and feed as the leash goes taut. Repeat the behavior until it is reliable.

12. Practice the behavior in a number of distracting environments:

    (a) Go for an off-leash walk with a friend and her dog (one that your dog knows and feels comfortable with).

    • Say your cue word.

    • Turn and run away from them.

    • Click and feed your dog for staying with you.

    • Repeat several times during the walk.

(b) Go to a public, on-leash park.

- Walk your dog on the perimeter.
- Say your cue word.
- Run in the opposite direction.
- Click and feed your dog for calm responses to your cue of turning quickly and exhibiting stress behavior.

Secrets of success:

- In the early stages of teaching this behavior, avoid having your dog exposed to other dogs and stressful events during training sessions.
- Make this behavior a game. Laugh and keep your voice light as you give your verbal cue to turn and run.
- Only turn and depart from an encounter when it is safe to do so. For example, if you see another dog off-leash, in the distance, sometimes the sight of a dog and handler moving quickly in the opposite direction—especially if you are running away—will induce the other dog to follow you.

CHAPTER 4

Canine Interaction:
A Foreign Language

If your dog is highly reactive toward other dogs, the reason may be simply because he doesn't speak their language. Dogs who are not fluent in "Dog" are unable to read canine body postures and gestures. They lack the ability to express their intentions accurately with their own body language. Because of this illiteracy, these dogs can misread another dog's actions—a bark, a glance, a step forward—as a threat, regardless of intent. A dog's natural response to a perceived threat is aggression. Another result of the highly reactive dog's canine "illiteracy" is that his body movements are often considered grossly exaggerated and unnecessarily intense by other dogs.

Is it possible to give reactive dogs language lessons? Can we teach reactive dogs how to communicate calmly and fluently with their own species? Is it effective to teach them these skills mechanically, just as easily as if we were teaching them any other behavior?

The answer to all of these questions is yes. We can improve the way our dogs interact with others if we focus on teaching them how to meet other dogs safely, slowly, and politely. Some dogs need our help in learning to have courage when faced with the rambunctious body movements of other dogs at play or off-leash. Specific pieces of behavior can be clicker trained individually, and then put on cue, so that we can have a dialogue with our dog while he is meeting and interacting with other dogs, like a coach signaling to his quarterback. In the process, dogs begin to learn their own language, tentatively at first, but with more confidence as their fluency grows.

Change the Behavior; the Emotions Will Follow

While emotions drive behavior, the reverse is also true: emotions follow physical expression, or behavior. In psychology, the practice of "smile therapy" advises clients to hold a smile on their faces, whether they feel like it or not. The theory is that even a forced smile washes away the emotions that prevent you from smiling, increasing your motivation and confidence. In other words, if you want to be happy, act happy. In addition, changing the consequences of a behavior can alter an emotional state. While the psychologists are concerned with human behavior, clicker training accomplishes both objectives for our dogs. We can teach our dogs to perform separate social behaviors on cue while interacting with other dogs. If these behaviors are solidly on cue, they can help them relax, and spark spontaneous appropriate interactions.

When I wanted Ben to meet other dogs, I knew I needed to teach him a behavior that would require moving toward other dogs. Another dog would become, for our purposes, a prop: an object that would provide a clickable opportunity. Targeting, or touching his nose to an object on cue, was a behavior that Ben already knew well. So I decided to teach Ben to target, or touch, another dog's nose or hindquarters on cue.

At first, Ben would touch the other dog, and immediately look to me for a click and treat. As we worked on the behavior, something exciting began to happen. Ben would touch the other dog, turn to me for a click and treat, and then turn back to the other dog, gently wagging his tail. Trying to contain my glee, I would calmly let the two dogs meet, clicking and praising Ben for each second that he exhibited acceptable behavior.

Originally the target-the-dog behavior was simply a cued behavior that Ben would perform in conjunction with the other dog. But as Ben discovered that being close to another dog had its benefits, his attitude toward the other dog changed. The door opened to the possibility that Ben could meet other dogs happily.

When you teach your dog to touch another dog's nose or hindquarters on cue, you ask him to focus on a task rather than on the other dog. He will first see the other dog as an opportunity to earn a click and a reward. He learns, "Interaction with the other dog is the means through which I get clicked." As your dog grows accustomed to touching other dogs, the encounters become self-reinforcing and evolve into genuine social interaction.

Don't rush into these training sessions. If your dog is a danger to other dogs and truly attacks them, these sessions may never be appropriate for him. With the violently aggressive dog, work on desensitizing him to the environment that he considers aversive and teach him a behavior incompatible with aggression, rather than focusing on his canine body language. Other less-aggressive dogs, however, may regain the ability to play with friends, to run off-leash, and to take part in the other joys of dog life, just by learning to speak "Dog."

Training Recipes: Acting Friendly

Meet Other Dogs on Cue—Friends

As your highly reactive dog becomes more comfortable around other dogs, reinforce him for simply meeting other dogs. Introduce a cue that indicates to your dog that it is okay to meet this particular dog standing in front of you. Some handlers introduce the word cue "Friend" just as their dog starts to sniff the other dog.

Teach these steps very slowly, arranging meetings with other dogs that are friendly, calm, and extremely tolerant. Safety is always paramount. Do not hesitate to muzzle your dog if you have any concern that he could injure the other dog.

A basket muzzle is the best type of muzzle to use because you can feed treats through it as your dog is being reinforced for acting appropriately with the other dog. Before using the muzzle as a training tool, desensitize your dog to it just as you would desensitize your dog to the head collar. Allow your dog to sniff the muzzle. Click and feed. Begin to put it on your dog. Click and feed. Bring the muzzle closer and closer to the dog's face. Click and feed. Practice this in successful approximations until you are holding the muzzle piece on your dog's mouth. As your dog begins to feel more comfortable with the muzzle, pull the straps up behind his head. Click and feed. Finally, fasten the straps, click and feed, and take the muzzle immediately off the dog. Build up the time that your dog has the muzzle on his face, clicking and feeding at each step.

Please note: If you have a dog that is not highly reactive but just needs more exposure to other dogs, arrange play dates with stable, nonreactive dogs. At first, do this with one dog at a time. Keep the sessions short, three to five minutes at a time. Since dogs tend to be better off-leash, go to a neutral, safe area where your dog and the other dog may romp and play freely. Muzzle your dog, if you feel it necessary. If at any time your dog is reactive, end the play session, and give your dog a two- or three-minute time-out. Your dog loses the opportunity to play with the other dog if his behavior is not appropriate.

Especially helpful when…

- You are in a public place where there are many other dogs and you would like your dog to be more relaxed if strange dogs introduce themselves to him.
- You want your dog to have more doggy friends.

How to make it happen:

1. Make a list of dogs with whom your dog feels comfortable, even if there are only one or two.
2. Arrange with another handler to have your dogs meet.
3. Work in a secure area where no other dogs might approach off-leash. Both handlers will decide beforehand on an "end of interaction" word like "Okay" or "Right here."
4. Leash both dogs.
5. Start circling toward each other in an arc-like pattern.
6. Click and feed the dogs, with each step, as they walk toward each other.
7. Slowly close up the arc, clicking and feeding each dog as the circle gets smaller. (Use praise as the reward if one of the dogs is food possessive.)
8. Let the dogs begin to notice each other.
9. As the dogs start to sniff each other, click and softly praise for appropriate behavior. Do not interrupt the interaction by feeding but rather give your verbal cues, such as "Easy" or "Nice," while the interaction is taking place. Try to keep your leash loose.
10. After ten seconds of sniffing, handlers call their dog back to them. Please note that, even if you get nervous and your leash tightens as you pull your dog away, this should not cause a problem if you have already taught your dog that a tight leash means calm (see page 87).
11. Click and feed for a job well done!

12. Repeat Steps 6 through 11, slowly increasing the amount of time that the dogs spend together. If the dogs seem very comfortable together after the sessions, feel free to end with a well-supervised play session.

Practice this sequence many times with dogs that your dog already likes before introducing a strange dog.

Meet Other Dogs on Cue — Strangers

Level I

1. Make sure that the dog you are introducing your highly reactive dog to is friendly, calm, and safe.
2. Discuss with the other dog's owner in advance how the introduction will be handled.
   - It is not absolutely necessary for the other handler to have a clicker and treats, but it would be nice for the "test" dog to be rewarded highly for this exposure as well.
   - Make sure that the other handler understands that when you say "okay" the interaction is done and both dogs must come and sit in front of their owner.
3. Practice in a neutral environment that is safe from other off-leash dogs.
4. Both dogs should be on leashes. Muzzle your dog if you feel it necessary. (This will make you feel more secure too!)
5. Before the introduction itself, walk the dogs in a straight line, facing the same direction (parallel walking). Dogs should be five to ten feet apart, and arranged as dog, handler, dog, handler.
   - Click and feed your dog anytime he notices the other dog and stays calm.
   - Do not walk the dogs toward each other
   - If you notice that your dog is tense around the other dog (showing aggressive

signs), then click and feed from a distance and end the session for that day. Achieve success wherever you can and end the session.

If the dogs have been warmed up and remain calm:

6. The dog and handler pairs can now walk toward each other, beginning about twenty or thirty feet away. Rather than walking directly toward each other, however, each pair should start on one side of an imagined circle and approach each other in an arc.

7. Click and feed the dogs as they walk slowly closer to each other.

8. Slowly close up the arc, clicking and feeding each dog as the circle becomes smaller. (Stop forward movement whenever the dogs eat their treats.)

9. Let the dogs begin to notice each other. Click and feed each look.

10. Monitor your dog's body signals. End the session, if necessary, before your dog's tension becomes a display of aggression.

11. When the dogs arrive at the same point in the circle, let them curve naturally around each other.

12. As the dogs start to sniff each other, give your verbal cues such as "Easy" or "Nice" while the interaction is taking place. (Remember to keep a loose leash.)

13. After ten seconds of sniffing, each handler clicks and calls his or her dog.

14. Ask the dogs to come and sit and give eye contact.

15. Click and feed for a job well done!

16. When your dog has reached this point, you might want to teach him to touch another dog's nose on cue. This will further reinforce a friendly greeting (see page 105).

17. Repeat Steps 6 through 10, slowly increasing the amount of time that the dogs spend together.

Level II

1. If the dogs seem fine together, take the nonaggressive dog off his leash. Please make sure, at this point, that you are in a fenced or enclosed area. (It is best to take the stable dog off his leash first because there's less of a chance that he will cause a problem. Chances are he will display a calm canine greeting to signal to your dog that he is not a threat, helping to put your reactive dog at ease.)

2. Allow your dog to follow the now-unleashed dog if he wants. Remember to keep your leash loose.

3. Click and praise for all appropriate canine behavior.

4. Allow this to happen for about ten seconds and, after ten seconds, have the other handler secure her dog.

5. Click and feed both dogs for great behavior!

6. Repeat Steps 1 through 5 until both dogs are fine.

Level III

1. Reintroduce the dogs in a safe, enclosed area.

2. Repeat the steps for Level I and Level II.

3. Now take your dog off the leash and allow the dogs to interact.

4. At first, allow the dogs to interact for small amounts of time only. Slowly lengthen the time that they are together.

5. At the end of each session, each handler calls his or her dog back to front.

6. The handlers click and feed their dog for coming to them, making sure to put their hand on the dog's collar for security.

7. At the end of the sessions, each handler puts his or her dog back on leash.

Please note: The more dogs your dog meets, the more dogs your dog will feel comfortable with. Once he's had enough practice, various scenarios will be a breeze for him to handle. For example, let's say you're in a training class and another dog sticks his face in your dog's face. You can quickly say "Friend" and your dog will relax and sniff back or simply look at you for a click and a treat. Bravo!

Secrets of success:

- Work slowly.
- It is better to work small successful sessions frequently, for example three days a week, than it is to work one small session once every two weeks.
- Always maintain a high rate of reinforcement.
- Make sure your dog knows his foundation behaviors, especially his recall.
- Teach your dog that a tight leash means calm.
- Always end the dog-to-dog interaction on a positive note and walk away.
- Our goal is always to get behavior and proactively prevent aggressive episodes from taking place.
- If ever your dog decides that he does not want to meet a dog, respect his decision and end the session.

Touch Another Dog's Nose or Hindquarters on Cue

You can teach your dog to introduce himself appropriately to another dog on cue; he does this by softly touching the other dog's nose or hindquarters. As he performs a canine greeting as a trained behavior, he will focus on the task rather than the stressful fact that another dog is in close proximity. The other dog becomes vital to the learning equation: "Interaction with another dog earns me a click."

Especially helpful when…

- You want your dog to become comfortable in close proximity to other dogs.
- You want to get your dog used to having other dogs sticking their nose in his face.

How to make it happen:

1. Work with another dog and handler. Pick a dog that your dog likes. If your dog is not comfortable with any dogs, see if you can find a handler with a nonreactive dog who would be willing to help.

2. Work in a secure area where no other unleashed dogs will interrupt the training session.

3. Leash both dogs.

4. Ask the other handler to stand in the center of the space with her dog at her side.

5. Start walking with your dog toward the other dog. Instead of walking straight up, curve in an arc around the other dog.

6. Click and feed after each step that takes you closer to the other dog.

7. Stop a couple of feet from the other dog.

8. Click and feed your dog for looking at the other dog.

9. Take another step closer.

10. Click and feed your dog as he sniffs the other dog. Note that each time you click, your dog will automatically look up at you again for his treat. Then say "okay" and begin again. If successful, repeat three to four times per session.

11. When your dog begins to start sniffing the other dog's nose or hindquarters on his own, you can now add the verbal cue "Touch." Reinforce your dog for sniffing the other dog's face (nose) only.

12. Practice this behavior with as many friendly, nonreactive dogs as you can. The more exercises you can do in and around other dogs, the more your dog will feel comfortable with dogs around him, especially if you have specific exercises where the other dog is part of the learning environment.

Secrets of success:

• If your dog has a hard time understanding that touching the other dog means a click and a treat, teach your dog how to target on everyday objects first. A canine stuffed animal is a great object to start with. (See the "Targeting" section on page 45.)

• It might be easier to start teaching your dog to touch another dog's hindquarters on cue first before advancing to touching the other dog's face. Sniffing the hindquarters of another dog is one of the first things dogs do when they meet each other.

• Follow the steps of this recipe a lot more slowly if your dog is interacting with a strange dog.

• Maintain a high rate of reinforcement.

• Make sure your dog has worked the "Meeting Other Dogs on Cue" exercises in the previous training recipe before progressing to this section.

• Safety first, always. Feel free to muzzle your dog when practicing this exercise.

• This skill comes in handy if another dog rudely introduces himself to your dog. Your dog will automatically think that this is part of an exercise. Your dog will remain calm, therefore you will remain calm.

• Click and feed your dog anytime another dog happens to stick his nose in your dog's face without incident. This is called "capturing the behavior" and will be an increasingly useful method to reinforce your dog's calm, spontaneous interactions with other dogs, as they become more frequent.

Desensitizing Your Dog to Other Dogs' Natural Responses

Once your dog feels comfortable in the presence of other dogs, teach him to start tolerating the "rude" behavior of more inquisitive dogs. Your dog can learn to tolerate another dog sniffing his tail or hindquarters, or another dog running into him head-on. Dogs that stare at him while he is in his kennel or dogs that slam into him haphazardly can be quite annoying, but your dog can learn to deal with these annoyances in a nonaggressive way.

The key to desensitizing your dog to these potentially volatile situations is to turn them into "clickable" events by clicking and treating your dog each time they happen. He will learn that the stressful event occurring means he should look to you immediately. Instead of your dog throwing himself aggressively at another dog, as he has done in the past, he will look up at you as if to say, "Did you see what just happened? Hey, Mom (or Dad), pay up now!"

This is how your dog learns that anytime something frightens him or makes him feel uncomfortable, his role is to give you his fullest attention, immediately. Then, you, as his leader, can make the appropriate decisions to keep him safe. The frightening episode, whatever it may be, becomes in itself the cue to relax and make immediate eye contact.

Once I had entered Ben in an obedience competition. We were in the ring practicing the long sit when, all of a sudden, there was a dogfight "two dogs down" from where Ben was sitting. As the ruckus began, you could actually see Ben's body tighten and strain forward until he looked like he was going to fall over. He stared hard into my eyes as he struggled to maintain his position. I clicked. Though my heart was in my mouth, I walked calmly to Ben and gave him a whole handful of treats. Job well done! By then both owners had regained control of their dogs and we went on to perform the long down successfully.

We know that your dog will never actually "like" these stressful occurrences; however, with patience and practice, you can effectively lower the reactivity level to almost nothing.

Begin by listing in your training journal all the canine behaviors you have witnessed that seem to set your dog off. Set up training sessions with a dog that your dog likes, clicking and feeding him as the noxious behavior occurs. These behaviors can include:

- Another dog sniffing your dog's hindquarters.
- Another dog staring at your dog while he is in his kennel.
- Another dog coming at your dog head-on (especially bad when dragging an irate owner at the end of the leash).
- Another dog trying to eat your dog's treat as you click and feed him.
- Another dog mistakenly slamming into your dog.
- Another dog mistakenly stepping over your dog.

The next few training recipes show you how to teach your dog to be tolerant of several of these common canine behaviors. They are followed by recipes for "Calming Signals," behaviors your dog can turn to when faced with a potentially volatile situation. Remember that when other dogs exhibit rude behaviors, they're not necessarily being aggressive; what makes the behavior a problem is if your dog perceives it as threatening. Follow the steps in these recipes, and you will help change your dog's perceptions of other dogs' behaviors: instead of seeing a threat, your dog will see an opportunity to look to you for a treat.

Read the description for each of the following training recipes. Begin each slowly. Work in one- to two-minute increments until your dog slowly builds up his tolerance level. Always use a high rate of reinforcement with treats that your dog absolutely adores.If your dog does not have any compatible canines with which to work, then be prepared to click and feed calm responses when they happen spontaneously. Your dog will still learn that another dog's rude behavior created a "clickable" moment for him.

Training Recipes:
Accepting "Rude" Dog Behavior

Another Dog Sniffs Your Dog's Hindquarters

This common canine "getting to know you" greeting can make some dogs nervous. You can teach your dog to tolerate another dog sniffing his hindquarters. When it happens, he will look up at you as if to say, "Look what happened! Time for a click and a treat!"

Especially helpful when...

- You are in a public place and many dogs are drifting past your dog. You always try to make sure that no other dog threatens your dog; however, every once in a while another dog can and will take a quick sniff. You want your dog to be prepared.

How to make it happen:

1. Pick a dog (and handler) your dog likes with whom to work.

2. Work in a secure area where no other unleashed dogs can interfere with your dog's training session.

3. Keep both dogs on leashes.

4. Use a very high rate of reinforcement.

5. Allow the other dog to come up and sniff your dog.

6. Click and feed your dog as the other dog approaches, especially if the other dog starts sniffing his hindquarters. (Make sure that as you click and feed your dog, the other handler either does the same or moves away with her dog. We do not want any food possession issues. It is nice if both dogs are getting treated at the same time.)

7. After rewarding both dogs, end the session and begin again.

8. Work this behavior with a variety of dogs that your dog already knows. Start practicing with a wider range of dogs only after your dog begins giving you eye contact when the sniffing starts with the first dog you're working with.

9. Work on this behavior with unfamiliar dogs.

10. When out in public, spontaneously click and feed your dog if any other dog sniffs his hindquarters or any other part of his body.

11. Repeat Steps 1 through 6.

Secrets of success:

•   Click and feed your dog for allowing any other dog to sniff his body, especially his tail or hindquarters, unexpectedly.

Your Dog Is Comfortable with Dogs Near His Kennel

Your dog's kennel should give him a sense of security. Teach him that being in his kennel keeps him safe from other dogs. No matter what behavior other dogs exhibit in and around his kennel, he can ignore them. The kennel is his own space and he is safe in there.

Especially helpful when…

•   You are in a place where there are other dogs. It could be a canine seminar or a family picnic. You need a break. You bring your portable kennel to put your dog in so that both you and your dog can take a rest.

How to make it happen:

1. Put your dog in his kennel in the middle of the room. A wire crate is best to use because it has openings all the way around.

2. Ask a friend to walk her dog near your dog's kennel.

3. Click and feed your dog generously in his kennel for calmly accepting each of the following elements:

    *   Proximity: How close can the other dog be? Begin to close the space so that eventually the other dog can walk right beside the kennel.

    *   Direction: At first work on your friend and her dog walking past your dog's kennel without any opportunity for eye contact between the two dogs. Then have them walk past the kennel, allowing for eye contact. Gradually work up to having the other handler and her dog walk all the way around your dog's kennel; then have them do laps around the kennel. Finally, have the other owner and her dog walk right up to the kennel, head-on.

    *   Speed: Walk the other dog past slowly. Speed up the pace of the dog until it is running past the kennel. Then have the dog run up to the kennel.

    *   Time: Slowly lengthen the amount of time that the other dog is ambling around the crate.

4. If at any time your dog explodes, back up. You went too far, too fast.

5. Once this behavior is solid, start having other dogs walk by, first one, then two, etc.

6. Find a local training class to which the instructor will allow you to take your dog and keep him in his kennel while other dogs walk past. Click and feed him for each dog that walks by him while he remains calmly in his kennel. Prepare properly for Step 6:

    *   Set up your crate first and then bring your dog in.

    *   Have your clicker and treats ready.

    *   Make sure you get your dog into his kennel before the environment gets too

crowded. Arrive fifteen minutes before class starts or fifteen minutes after the class begins.

- Avoid getting caught with your dog in any tight doorways with other dogs that he doesn't know.
- If you need a break, do not leave your dog in his kennel by himself. When the environment has quieted down, put him back in your car when you are not working with him.

7. Continue working this behavior in many different environments.

Secrets of success:

- Click and feed your dog anytime he does not react when another dog walks by his crate. You can also click and feed him for the lessening of aggressive behaviors exhibited when another dog walks by.

Dogs Approaching Your Dog Head-On

When another dog approaches your dog head-to-head, it does not have to be an intimidating event; you can teach your dog to take it in stride. Eventually, your dog should even be able to handle other dogs approaching quickly. Instead of creating panic, your dog will react by making immediate eye contact with you.

Especially helpful when…

- You are walking your dog in a town square. As you are walking, another dog owner allows her dog to pull her over to say "hello" right in your dog's face.

How to make it happen:

1. Work with a handler and dog that your dog likes.
2. Work in a secure area where no other unleashed dogs will interrupt the training session.

3. Keep both dogs on leashes with their handlers.

4. Sit your dog on your left.

5. Ask your dog to watch you. (See the eye contact exercises on pages 38–40.)

6. Ask the other handler to slowly walk her dog up to yours head-on (in a straight line) while your dog is watching you, sitting on your left. You can also have both dogs walking slowly toward each other. Make sure to keep a comfortable distance, ten feet or so, between the two dogs as they approach each other.

7. Click and feed your dog for each step taken by the other dog as the other dog approaches.

8. Once the dog is in close proximity, have the handler continue walking past you quietly.

9. Make sure to continue clicking and feeding your dog when the visiting dog is closest.

10. Withhold reinforcement as the dog is moving away.

11. Repeat the previous steps with several familiar dogs.

12. As your dog becomes more comfortable with this exercise, allow him to break eye contact with you and watch the other dog as he approaches.

13. Click and feed your dog as the other dog moves closer.

14. Based on your prior work, what will happen is that your dog will see the other dog approaching and then will look up at you in anticipation of the click and treat. Once you have rewarded your dog, say "okay" and allow your dog to look at the other dog again.

15. Repeat Steps 6 through 11.

16. Remember to work on one piece of the behavior at a time. If you are working with a new dog, go back to Step 1.

17. Continue working on this behavior with strange dogs approaching but never really meeting your dog.

18. Increase the speed at which the other dog approaches.

Secrets of success:

- Click and feed your dog for silence and calm anytime another dog walks up to him head-on. Feel free to click and feed your dog, give your release word, and move to a more secure area. Your dog will see nothing peculiar about moving away as long as you have desensitized him to this element ahead of time.

Dogs Eating Treats Together

We want our dogs to get used to being clicked and fed in the company of other dogs. Follow these steps to teach your dog that he doesn't have to worry that any nearby dogs will steal his treat when he's getting clicked and treated.

Especially helpful when...

You are working with your dog in a crowded environment. You want to reinforce your dog, but some of the other dogs are in close proximity. You do not want your dog to react to the other dogs around him as you give him the treat that he has earned.

How to make it happen:

1. Put your dog in a sit/stay about five feet from another dog. The other dog's handler follows these same steps. Both dogs are on leash.
2. Tell your dog to stay, and step out, toe-to-toe, in front of your dog.
3. Click and feed your dog five times from the front position. After each click and treat, remember to re-cue your dog to stay.
4. After you've given the fifth treat, swing back to your dog's left. Click and feed.
5. End the session.
6. Continue to practice these "baby" stays as you move the dogs closer and closer, approximately a half a foot at a time. Try to work with the same dog as you make this exercise more challenging.

7. Eventually the dogs will be doing sit/stays side by side, each accepting his own set of treats.

8. Once your dog is successful with the side-by-side sit/stays, ask your dog for sit/stays next to the other dog at varied and unexpected intervals (preferably the same one you have been working with), and click and feed your dog for staying.

9. Ask your dog to stay, click and feed your dog first, and then click and feed the other dog.

10. Click and feed your dog for tolerating this behavior.

11. Slowly build this behavior with one dog, then two, then three, and so on.

12. As your dog's experience grows, ask him to sit/stay next to unfamiliar dogs. Repeat Steps 1 through 10. Use a basket muzzle so that you are still able to feed your dog treats.

Secrets of success:

• Click and feed your dog anytime he is around other dogs. Every once in a while, ask your dog to sit/stay (click and feed for this) while you click and feed a neighbor's dog, making sure that your dog and the strange dog remain sitting.

• Prepare for this exercise beforehand by perfecting the "Stay" from the Foundation Behaviors section in Chapter 2. (See page 45.)

Other Dogs Bumping into Your Dog

It's bound to happen: sometimes dogs just bump into each other. Whether this occurs when the handlers are jostling for position or when the dogs are playing off-leash, you can desensitize your dog to this incidental contact with other dogs.

Especially helpful when...

• You are working with your dog in a crowded environment or walking where other dogs are playing. Even if another dog should physically touch your dog, you want to make sure that your dog will not react aggressively under your guidance.

How to make it happen:

1. Work with a handler and dog that your dog likes.

2. Work in a secure area where no other unleashed dogs will interrupt the training session.

3. Keep both dogs on leashes with their handlers.

4. Practice in short sessions—five minutes at the most.

5. Maintain a high rate of reinforcement.

6. Have your dog either sit/stay or stand/stay.

7. Have the other handler walk by you with her dog.

8. Click and feed your dog as the other dog and its handler walk toward you.

9. As the other handler walks by you and your dog, have her walk her dog extremely close to your dog.

10. Click and feed your dog when the two dogs are at their closest.

11. Next have the other handler walk her dog so close to yours that her dog actually brushes (gently) against your dog.

12. Click and feed your dog right at this moment.

13. Repeat Steps 5 through 12 until your dog is completely calm. Click and treat for eye contact as well.

14. Next, increase the amount of pressure exerted on your dog as the other dog brushes by him. Work with what is reasonable.

15. Now that your dog is comfortable with this dog touching him, practice Steps 5 through 13 at a quicker pace.

16. As your dog's behavior becomes increasingly reliable, start working this behavior with an unfamiliar dog. Use a basket muzzle, if needed, so that you can still feed your dog treats.

17. Continue to increase the level of exposure with one dog, then two, then three, and so on.

Secrets of success:

• "Catch" the behavior and reinforce it by clicking and feeding your dog anytime another dog touches him, moves toward him, etc.

• Expose your dog to nearby dogs for small amounts of time.

• Watch your dog's position in the environment intently.

• Remember, you need to be able to control the environment, and your dog's reaction to it, at all times. Do not take your dog to an environment where dogs are running off-leash until your dog is ready for this level of exposure.

Other Dogs Stepping over your Dog

Your dog doesn't have to react aggressively if another dog walks over his tail or otherwise enters his personal space; you can teach him to remain calm should such an encounter take place.

Especially helpful when…

• You are with your dog in an obedience class. You are waiting for the class to start. Your dog is lying calmly by your side. Another handler, who came in late with her dog, heels her dog forward, not realizing that your dog's tail is in the way. You try to reposition your dog, but just as your dog is getting up, the other dog trips over his body. Instead of blowing up, your dog looks at you as if to say, "Look what happened! Pay up!" Disaster averted!

How to make it happen:

1. Work in a controlled environment.

2. Start out working with a dog that your dog already likes.

3. If your dog does not have a doggy friend, either follow the "Secrets of Success" tip at the end of this training recipe or first teach your dog to meet a stable, nonreactive dog by following the instructions on page 102, "Meeting Other Dogs on Cue—Strangers." Then move on to Step 4.

4. Keep your dog on-leash.

5. Down your dog.

6. Ask him to stay.

7. Position yourself in front of your dog, clicker and treats in hand.

8. Ask the handler of the other dog to walk in a straight line, a short distance from your dog's tail, in one direction only.

9. Click and feed your dog as the other dog walks by his tail.

10. Repeat steps 8 and 9 until your dog reliably remains calm.

11. As your dog gets used to the dog moving behind him, now ask the handler to walk her dog over the tip of your dog's tail.

12. Click and feed as your dog tolerates this.

13. Slowly, and only with success, ask the handler to walk her dog higher and higher up on your dog's tail.

14. Click and feed for compliance.

15. As your dog becomes more and more comfortable in this position, have the handler increase the speed at which she and her dog move.

Secrets to success:

•   Click and feed your dog anytime another dog steps over his tail or another part of his body. This is a nice exercise to practice in a class regardless of whether or not your dog knows the other dogs. I call this "Doggy Limbo."

Calming Signals

Dogs constantly exhibit signals, or signs, in the form of facial expressions and body movements. The signal is given, then received and interpreted by the other individual in the environment; with the signal, the signal giver may influence the behavior of the other. Signals vary; some invite interaction, some threaten and say "back off."

Calming signals, a term first used by Norwegian behavioral scientist Turid Rugaas, describes signals that a tentative dog might use to "calm" his surroundings. The dog uses these signals to communicate to the other animal that he (the signal giver) is not a threat; he's also looking for a similar appeasing gesture in response from the other dog. In order to calm himself down, the dog may choose to use a behavior that he enjoys and therefore finds a greater sense of security while performing it.

Calming signals in dogs can include licking the lips or nose, turning the head, play bowing, yawning, sitting, downing, body shake, scratching, turning a part or the whole body away, walking slowly, freezing or becoming motionless, sniffing, and lifting a paw. (If a dog displays one of these behaviors, however, he may not be using it as calming signal. A dog will, for example, sniff the grass whether or not there is a threat in the environment.)

In most dogs these avoidance behaviors occur naturally; however, the reactive dog often has no idea how to use his own set of calming signals and in what situation. Many of these dogs cannot even visually recognize these signals in another dog when they are confronted with them. At this point, they still consider any body movement to be a threat.

Through clicker training, we can teach our dogs calming signals, one at a time, to be used when in an appropriate situation. Please note that I am not suggesting that we try to "mind read" when dogs are freely interacting with each other, but rather to teach these signals to our reactive dogs in the hopes that they will "rediscover" them and naturally begin using them on their own. There is no reason that, when our dogs are safely with us on a leash, we cannot teach them what behaviors are within the range of appropriate responses to another dog's behavior.

For example, when you are clicking and feeding your dog for merely looking at another dog, your dog will turn to look at you for a click and a treat. At that moment, by turning his head, your dog is also sending a message to the other dog that he is not a threat. You are also teaching your dog the calming signal of turning his head away.

You can teach your dog a variety of calming signals separately to help support your dog in a stressful situation. In doing this, you are not only teaching your dog how to calm another dog (or person) in a given circumstance by his body movements, but you are also teaching your dog how to calm himself as well. Remember, change the behavior and the emotions will follow. Initially, these behaviors are singularly taught and handler-cued; however, as your dog builds more confidence, and becomes more skilled at exhibiting these signs, he will tend to spontaneously use them. Though the reason for this is uncertain, we see this pattern continually repeat itself.

It is a good idea to observe and study these canine signals in the interactions of emotionally healthy dogs, first, so that you will be able to easily recognize them and reinforce them as your dog begins to experiment. It also helps to videotape your dog in the many different environments within which he is active. For example, you might want to record him when he is meeting new people and meeting new dogs. You could also videotape him playing with other dogs at the dog park and when he is playing with other dogs at home. Note the differences. Play the tape back in slow motion. Become familiar with your dog's body language. The more accurately you can read his body language, the more you can reinforce preferred behavior and the more responsive you will be in filling in the "weak" spots with confidently cued behaviors.

Training Recipes: Using Calming Signals

Sniffing the Ground

When your dog bends his head down to sniff the ground, other dogs perceive it as a submissive posture. It is helpful to put this behavior on cue. Then you can cue your dog to begin sniffing the ground when another dog and handler approach.

Especially helpful when...

- Your dog is reactive with strangers. A neighbor approaches as you are walking your dog. You cue your dog to sniff the ground as you and your neighbor have a quick discussion. (A sit, another calming signal, would work here as well, as long as the dog's stay behavior is reliable.)

How to make it happen:

1. Sprinkle several pieces of kibble on the ground.
2. As your dog begins to eat each piece, one by one, click.
3. Once the dog finishes, he will continue to scour the ground for more crumbs.
4. As he does this, click for each drop of his head, and drop a treat on the ground.
5. Continue to click and feed, as he stays interested in what is underfoot.
6. Practice this sequence three or four times, approximately ten clicks a session.
7. Slowly lengthen the time that your dog is sniffing the ground.
8. Now that he is actively sniffing, attach a verbal cue to the behavior.
9. Ask him to sit/stay or stand/stay, give him his cue to sniff, and as he drops his head, click and throw a treat on the ground.
10. Practice this behavior in a variety of environments.
11. Vary the surfaces that your dog will drop his head to.
12. When this behavior becomes reliable, ask a friend to walk her dog on a leash.
13. As your dog alerts, cue your dog to begin to sniff.
14. Click and throw treats on the ground for compliance.

Secrets of success:

- "Catch" the behavior and reinforce it by clicking and feeding your dog anytime he drops his head in response to another dog or person approaching. Throw the treats on the ground after you click so that the dog's focus remains elsewhere. If another dog is too close by, you might want to either praise your dog or hand-feed him as he sniffs.

Freeze in a Sit

Once you've taught your dog to stay absolutely still as another dog sniffs him, you can use the behavior to defuse what could be a volatile situation.

Especially helpful when...

- You are walking your dog and another dog, off-leash, runs up to yours. Your dog freezes in a sit/stay position as the other dog's owner struggles to get him under control.

How to make it happen:

1. Work with a dog and handler your dog is comfortable with. If there are no dogs that your dog gets along with, then proceed to Steps 11 and 12.
2. Work in a secure area where no other unleashed dogs can interfere with your dog's training session.
3. Keep both dogs on leashes.
4. Ask your dog to sit and stay.
5. Allow the other dog to come up and sniff your dog's hindquarters.
6. Click and feed your dog as the other dog sniffs him. Use a very high rate of reinforcement. If you cannot feed your dog around the other dog, simply click and praise your dog as the sniffing is taking place.
7. At the end, say "okay" and release both dogs.

8. Repeat Steps 4 through 7, making sure your dog stays "frozen" in the sit position as he is being sniffed.

9. As your dog gets used to having the other dog sniff him, give your dog a verbal cue that means "sit and don't move!"

10. If possible, work this behavior with a variety of dogs that your dog already knows.

11. As your dog becomes more successful, work on this behavior with unfamiliar dogs.

   • Use a muzzle if necessary.

   • When out in public, spontaneously click and feed your dog if any other dog sniffs his hindquarters or any other part of his body.

12. Repeat Steps 4 through 7.

Secrets of success:

• "Catch" and reinforce the behavior by clicking and feeding your dog for allowing any other dog to sniff his body, especially his tail or hindquarters, unexpectedly. As the dog begins to sniff, make sure to give your dog the sit signal.

Lift a Front Paw

Lifting a paw is a sign of deference. If your dog is concentrating on lifting his paw or giving his paw when he meets new people, it will help him stay calm.

Especially helpful when...

• Your dog is not good with strangers. You are at the park and you see a friend you haven't seen in years. Quickly he or she approaches. Ask your dog to sit/stay, and have him lift a front paw for added concentration.

How to make it happen:

1. Work in a quiet area.

2. Have clicker and tasty treats ready.

3. Ask your dog to sit and stay.

4. Click and feed for compliance.

5. Watch your dog's front feet.

6. Click and feed for any movement. After you click, toss the treat so that your dog has to get up to get it.

7. Begin again.

8. If you need to get the dog started, take a treat and lure the dog into shifting the position of his front feet.

9. Click and treat any lift or movement of his foot, however tiny.

10. Continue to click as paw movements become more pronounced.

11. Click for the higher paw movements while ignoring the lower ones.

12. As your dog begins to lift his paw, intentionally put your hand in the way.

13. Click as his paw touches your hand.

14. Repeat several times.

15. Now move your hand so the dog has to target your hand with his paw. Move your hand left, right, above your dog's head, and below your dog's head.

16. Click and treat for all successful paw touches.

17. Now that your dog is practicing this behavior, add your verbal cue as you hold out your hand.

18. Click and treat as your dog gives you his paw.

19. Practice this behavior in a variety of circumstances and environments.

Secrets of success:

• Click and feed your dog anytime he spontaneously greets a person or another dog with a lifted paw.

Turning His Back While in the Kennel

Your dog might get anxious when he's in his kennel and another dog approaches. If you teach him to turn his back to the kennel door, he can use the behavior to calm himself and to show the other dog he is not looking for a confrontation.

Especially helpful when…

- You are taking a class in a crowded training building and many of the beginner students do not have control over their rambunctious dogs. Several dogs pull their owners over to your crate. Smartly, your formerly reactive dog sees them coming, gets up, and lies with his back to the front of his crate. Disinterested, the other dogs leave.

How to make it happen:

1. Work in a distraction-free area.
2. Have clicker, target stick, delicious treats, and wire crate on hand. (You can purchase a target stick or simply use a wooden dowel or ruler.)
3. Stick one of your treats on the end of the target stick.
4. When your dog starts to sniff the end of the stick, click and treat.
5. Repeat this behavior a few times.
6. Now present the target stick without the treat on the end.
7. Click and treat your dog for touching the stick in any way.
8. As your dog begins to readily touch the stick, assign a verbal cue such as "Touch" to the behavior. Give your verbal cue right before the behavior happens.
9. Start to vary the position of the target stick: position it above your dog's head and below it, and to the left or to the right of your dog's face. Click as the dog's head turns to touch the stick. Then hold the stick a couple of feet away from your dog, and click and feed as your dog moves forward to touch the stick. Gradually widen the distance.
10. Heighten the challenge of touching the stick; ask your dog to touch it in a vari-

ety of different environments and circumstances. Then put your dog in his wire crate and begin working the behavior from there: Present the target stick, and as your dog goes to try and touch it, while he's in the crate, click and treat.

11. Now that your dog is touching the stick reliably on cue, add the 180-degree turn. First teach your dog this behavior when he is not in his crate.

    • Click and feed, in smaller increments, as your dog turns his body to touch the stick.

    • Continue having your dog turn his body until he is facing in the opposite direction.

    • As this becomes one fluid movement, assign a verbal cue such as "Turn" or "Around" to the behavior.

12. Repeat Step 12(c) until your dog is turning around easily.

13. Now fade the visual cue so that your dog will perform it on a verbal cue only. Begin by fading the target stick. Continue to use it but make it shorter and shorter. Present the ever-shrinking target stick and tell your dog to "Turn." Slowly begin to separate the two cues, relying increasingly on the verbal cue and only using the physical cue (the target stick) when necessary.

14. Practice this turning behavior when your dog is in his wire crate.

15. Once your dog responds reliably to the "Turn" cue, bring him to a place where there are dogs on-leash.

16. Put him in his wire crate.

17. Stand to the side of the crate, toward the back. Stand so that when you tell your dog to "Turn," he will turn his body toward you. In that way he can give you eye contact as well if needed.

18. Ask a handler to walk toward your crate with her dog.

19. As your dog alerts to the other dog moving in his direction, tell your dog to "Turn." Go back to using the target stick initially if you need to.

20. As your dog turns toward where you are standing, click and throw a handful of treats into the kennel.

21. Continue to practice this behavior until it is reliable.

Secrets of success:

• When your dog is in his crate and there are lots of other dogs around, sit in a chair behind his kennel, and click and feed him for any behavior that is calm and nonresponsive to the other dogs. Click him for any attention he gives you as well, especially if he turns and lies down facing you with his back to the opening of the kennel, hence ignoring the other dogs.

Play Bow

Dogs commonly use a bow or a stretch to say "Let's play!" Teach your dog to perform this behavior on cue, and you can summon the behavior when you want to encourage a playful or relaxed mood.

Especially helpful when...

• Your dog usually gets along fine with other dogs once they have been formally introduced. He has the habit, though, of puffing up and trying to take control of the situation at first; then he invites play and both dogs interact. Instead of allowing this sequence of events to play out, briefly introduce the dogs, then cue the play bow to see if this will initiate play sooner.

• Your dog is in a stressful environment. Find a quiet place and cue your dog to stretch into a play bow for relaxation purposes.

How to make it happen:

1. Work in a distraction-free area.

2. Have clicker, target stick, and delicious treats on hand. (You can purchase a target stick or simply use a wooden dowel or ruler.)

3. Stick one of your treats on the end of the target stick.

4. When your dog starts to sniff the end of the stick, click and treat.

5. Repeat this behavior a few times.

6. After your dog is reliably touching the target stick, ask him to stand.

7. Put the target stick in front of your dog's nose.

8. Click and treat for the touch.

9. Work this target-touching behavior through five to six repetitions, gradually dropping the end of the target stick to the floor between attempts.

10. Click and feed your dog for touching the end of the stick each time. Your dog should still be standing.

11. Now place the end of the target stick on the floor between your dog's front feet.

12. Click and feed as your dog bends down and touches the end of the stick.

13. In three to four repetitions, slowly move the end of the stick between your dog's front feet, pushing the stick under the dog and farther back toward his tail each time.

14. Click and feed as your dog begins to arch his back to touch the end of the stick.

15. Continue working this behavior until your dog is presenting a play bow.

16. Once your dog is bowing readily, add the verbal cue by saying "Bow" just before he begins the behavior.

17. Begin to fade the target stick by using your hand instead of the stick to cue the behavior.

18. Generalize this behavior by practicing it in different environments.

Please note: At no time should you ask your dog to play bow to a strange dog, as it would be asking the dog to display the behavior in an unnatural way. Bowing is to be used as a stress reliever or to initiate play with a dog that your dog knows and enjoys.

Secrets of success:

• "Catch" the behavior and reinforce it when it occurs spontaneously: When your dog happily and playfully bows to another dog, click and treat (or simply praise if the play behavior is already underway). You can also click and feed your dog for stretching when he gets up in the morning.

Slow Motion

Slow, smooth movements are incompatible with fast, knee-jerking aggressive reactions. Teach your dog to perform all his obedience behaviors in slow motion, especially the heeling sequence; this could help you make a smooth exit from a sticky situation.

Especially helpful when…

• There are a lot of noisy dogs in the environment. Have your dog move very slowly as he performs his heel and other obedience tasks, which will help him focus on his behaviors.

• There has just been a dog fight in your corner of the room. Though both dogs are now safely with their owners, you still want to get your dog out of there. You quietly pack up your belongings and slowly exit the building with your dog, not wanting to rouse further nasty sentiments.

How to make it happen:

1. Work in a distraction-free area.
2. Have clicker and delicious treats ready to go.
3. Follow the instructions for "Heeling on a Loose Leash" on page 43.
4. Practice all of the steps listed for "Heeling on a Loose Leash" but in slow motion: move slowly while walking next to your dog and click and reinforce him for keeping pace with you.

5. Increase your rate of reinforcement, if necessary, to maintain the dog's attention.

6. Practice these slow movements in a variety of different environments.

7. Feel free to practice all of your dog's other obedience behaviors in slow motion as well.

8. Be creative if needed. At home, try practicing in time to some slow music. Call your dog to you, attach the leash to his collar, and begin slow-motion heeling. Click and feed your dog for remaining on your left side.

Secrets of success:

• Click and feed your dog for any behavior that is done slowly, especially while in the presence of other dogs. Slowing down is much more relaxing than rushing forward. As your dog becomes more trusting in his environment, he will begin to relax. Frenzied, frightened behavior will become a thing of the past. Help him practice tranquility by teaching him to move his body slowly.

Get Close

Once you have this "Get Close" behavior reliably on cue, you can ask your dog to turn with you when you turn away from a real or perceived threat in the environment.

Especially helpful when...

• You are in an environment with other dogs. All of a sudden, one of the nearby dogs starts growling at your dog. You want to turn your dog's body to the side to avoid a direct confrontation. Say "Get close" as your dog follows your cue to turn one quarter to the right.

How to make it happen:

1. Work in a distraction-free area.

2. Have clicker and delicious treats ready to go.

3. Attach a six-foot leash to your dog's collar.

4. Ask your dog to sit at your left side.

5. Standing in the same spot, pivot one-quarter turn to the right, bringing your dog with you.

6. As your dog moves into the position on your left, click and treat. (Treat your dog while he is sitting on your left.)

7. Repeat Steps 5 and 6 until your dog's transitions are smooth.

8. Once the behavior is reliable, add a verbal cue such as "Get close."

9. Take your dog to different environments where dogs are on-leash.

10. Cue your dog to "Get close" and turn as dogs are walking past.

11. Click and feed for success.

Secrets of success:

•   "Catch" the behavior and reinforce it whenever it happens spontaneously: Click and feed your dog anytime he adjusts his body in some way to a dog that might seem threatening to him.

CHAPTER 5

Clicker Home Management for the Multiple-Dog Household

Owning several dogs can be quite a challenge, especially if one of the dogs does not get along well with the others. Precautions can be taken to ensure that all dogs in the household remain happy and safe. Your role as a responsible dog owner is to evaluate each dog as an individual, and determine exactly what he or she needs to live a happy and well-adjusted life.

Regardless of the canine group hierarchy that exists, you, the owner and handler, need to be the leader of your pack. You are the top dog. Your relationship with each dog needs to be more powerful and influential than the bonds that exist between the dogs.

It is always a good idea to implement the clicker home management principles (see pages 17) with each of your dogs. The issues addressed in this chapter will help you customize your home-management training plan for a multiple-dog household. Follow the advice here and you will be able to manage your dogs' interactions while teaching them other appealing and helpful behaviors.

Be sure to work with your dogs both individually and in a group. It is very important that all of the dogs' interactions are always set up to succeed. Make a list of all the activities that the dogs love to do together, and under your thoughtful guidance, continue to allow them to practice these successful encounters. The more they can enjoy each other's company and practice calm behavior, the less reactive they will be. Some of these activities might include going for walks, going for car rides, sleeping in bed together, and so on.

If there have been aggressive episodes between certain dogs in the past, make a list of those as well. Evaluate each situation and determine the cause if you can. See if you can change the logistics of the situation to discourage the aggressive behavior from occurring again. For example, it could be that your dogs get along fine as long as they do not squeeze through the door in the morning in a mad rush to eliminate. Instead of allowing them to charge through the door all at once, cue the dogs to sit and stay until you call each dog by name. Release the dogs one by one, in the order that you choose. This will help to eliminate the aggressive behavior at the door.

Observe your dogs and interrupt any interactions that appear threatening. Don't wait until a fight breaks out before stepping in. It's up to you to keep order in your household—whether you have one dog or five. The following sections discuss aspects of training that are particularly important in a multiple-dog household. Review this information, work on the behaviors with your dogs, and keeping the peace should be as easy as 1, 2, 3.

"Saying Please"

Teaching your dog to "say please" is the first behavior discussed in the Ten Principles of Clicker Home Management presented in Chapter 1. The importance of this skill applies doubly (or more!) to the multiple-dog household. All of the dogs in your care should learn to work for their rewards. Just as we raise our children to be polite and respectful of others, we must also teach our dogs to maintain self-control and be gentle with the humans in the family, as well as with the other pets. We accomplish this by asking our dogs to "say please" by performing a specific behavior (a sit works well here) before we give them any kind of reward such as feeding, praising, or petting.

Name Recognition

Each dog should give you his full attention whenever you call his name. If your dogs each know their names, you may be able to prevent an aggressive interaction from ever taking place. You can interrupt the behavior simply by calling the name of the dog that is behaving aggressively. Teach name recognition with each dog separately before you use it in a group situation.

To teach your dog to recognize his name, say his name and then click and feed. He will soon begin to look at you in anticipation of a click and treat every time you say his name. Do not ask your dog to perform a specific behavior other than the voluntary eye contact. Generalize this behavior by working in as many different environments as you can.

During feeding time, ask all of the dogs to sit while you prepare the meals. You should feed each dog in a separate spot. Release each of the dogs, one by one, by saying his name and bringing him to his personal feeding location. Set the bowl down in front of him. Secure this area so that the other dogs cannot steal the meal. For example, if you are feeding dog number one in a crate, close the door of the crate. If you are feeding dog number two in a room, either close the door or put up a baby gate as you leave the area. If the other dogs follow you, say nothing and bring the remaining dogs back to their original location. Ask them to sit and repeat the exercise. Repeat until all of the dogs have been fed.

By following this ritual, order is maintained and fights are prevented. Each dog hears his name clearly and positively twice a day. It won't be long before each dog will wait his turn to have his meal delivered in his specific spot.

It is also helpful to be able to call dogs, one by one, through potentially "dangerous" areas such as narrow doorways or threatening thresholds. If you can, choreograph each of your dog's movements in and out of the small spaces within your home environment; call them by name and have them negotiate the passage individually. In this way you will prevent what could become aggressive interactions.

You can also teach your dogs to respond as a group. For example, when I want all of my dogs to pay attention, I will give the cue, "All dogs!" To teach this: Have all of the dogs perform a sit/stay. Say "All dogs," click once, and give each dog a treat. Do not throw the treat on the floor but rather deliver it to their mouths.

The cue "All dogs!" is helpful when all of the dogs need to move together as a group. For example, if there is an emergency and you need to get them out of the house quickly, say "All dogs!" and they will come from their respective locations and will follow you wherever you lead. This cue is also handy if you are taking the dogs to the park and want them to enter or exit the van all at once. You can also use it as a precursor before another cue, such as "All dogs, come" or "All dogs, sit."

Foundation Behaviors

The more clicker-trained behaviors you can teach each of your dogs, the more versatility you will have in choreographing their successful interactions. To begin, work with each dog in a separate, distraction-free area. Introduce the clicker and begin working on one or two foundation behaviors at a time. Foundation behaviors include sits, downs, stays, heeling, come when called, hold an object, name recognition, four on the floor, and leave it.

Stationing

You will encounter many situations in which you will want to separate your dogs quickly. It is useful therefore to teach each dog to go to a particular place on cue. Ideally, you can teach your dog to go to this location and maintain a specific body position—a sit/stay or a down/stay, for example. Let's say you're going to do some kind of grooming of one of the dogs. The last thing you want is to have several dogs crowding the timid dog as he is getting his ears cleaned. To avoid this, send your dogs to their individual stations and have a family member or friend reinforce each dog for remaining calm and quiet, in his or her space, while the other dog is being groomed.

This cue is helpful even in the most trying of times. If the dogs should get into a squabble, tell each dog to go to his individual station and perform a down/stay until further notice. In this case, make sure the dogs' stations are far enough apart from each other to give them a sense of security, but close enough to be within eyesight. We want to make sure that each dog knows that he is being treated in the same fashion as the other. There are no "winners" to their disagreements; and you don't play favorites.

To teach this stationing behavior, first decide where each of your dogs will go upon hearing the station cue. For example, they might go to their individual crates or specified rooms. Then decide which word(s) will be your cue to tell them to go to their respective "houses." I use the words "Go kennel." Begin feeding your dog in the area that you have chosen to be his "station." He will begin to equate this area with being fed. Then wait until your dog runs into his space (he will be anticipating being fed), and just as he enters his station, say your cue word, click, and put down his meal. Repeat this behavior with each of your dogs individually.

When each of the dogs has the stationing behavior on cue, then you can say, for example, "All dogs, go kennel," and all of your dogs should run into their individual spaces.

If you want to refine this behavior even more you can also train the dogs to maintain a particular body position while in their special space. You can teach this just as you would any other foundation behavior. The only difference is that the dog remains in the crate while you shape the behavior.

Team Dynamics

As your dogs become more skilled in individual behaviors, begin to work two of them together in the same room. Start with the dogs far apart and slowly close up the space between them. Have another member of the family or a friend work with one dog as you work with the other. Use a muzzle if you think it's necessary. Work the dogs together but ask them to perform different exercises. For example, have one dog practice a sit/stay while the other dog heels past. Or have a small dog safely perform a sit/stay on a table while the larger dog practices a down/stay underneath the table. Click and feed each dog for success. Help them to work as a team. Slowly integrate any other dogs you may have, repeating this procedure. Just be sure that you work the dogs into the clicker training sessions one at a time.

When I was teaching Ben how to hold his dumbbell, the other dogs would position themselves around him and watch. When Ben held his dumbbell successfully, I would click him for the correct behavior, feed him, and then feed the other dogs for their respectful observance. All the dogs had a job. Each was focused on his individual task, even if it was something as simple as quietly maintaining self-control.

Be as creative as possible when working with your dogs as a group. Set up some training games so that the dogs can "play" with each other using their clicker-trained foundation behaviors. For example, ask one of the dogs to retrieve an object and put it into a box while the other dog watches and remains in a sit. Next, cue the first dog to sit and stay while the second dog goes to the box and retrieves the item and gives it to you. Look for many variations that will challenge you and your dogs.

Instilling a playful aspect to your dogs' group dynamics can definitely change the dogs' impressions of one another. The intra-group relationships, formerly based on competitiveness, now are based on compliance and cooperation.

Monitor Play Behavior

It's crucial that you keep an eye on your dogs when they are playing. Interrupt the play behavior if it gets out of hand or becomes violent. Remember, there is a fine line between overstimulation and aggression. Think of two little children. They might play physically by wrestling and pinning each other down. One child, unbeknownst to the other, winces in pain as his ankle smacks into the coffee table. Hurt and frustrated, he pulls the hair of the child who is on top of him. That child, in turn, hits the other for deliberately hurting him. The seemingly innocent play has now turned into an all-out brawl.

Dogs interact in very much the same way. They can start out playing nicely, but as the tension gets higher, and the time together grows longer, the play behavior can quickly spiral into aggression. Watch your dogs as they interact. Click and feed them (or click and praise them if one of the dogs is food aggressive) for all appropriate calm behavior. Allow them to play only when you can supervise.

Time-Outs

If any dog in your household begins to show threatening behaviors to another dog, then that aggressive dog should lose the opportunity to be with you and his canine companions. Silently remove the problem dog from the situation immediately and put him in a separate room. Either close the door or put up a strong barrier that the dog cannot climb over or push through. Leave him in there for no more than three minutes. Allow the dog to come out only after he is quiet.

Dog Fights

If a fight should break out, separate the dogs as quickly and safely as possible. It is usually best to grab them by the hind legs or tails and attempt to pull them apart. Don't grab their collars; stay away from their head and neck areas. It is not uncommon for dogs, in their frenzy, to whip their heads around and sink their teeth into their owner's skin accidentally.

You might also try throwing cold water on the dogs or spraying them with a hose if you are outside. Loud noises, like an air horn, can also interrupt a fight.

After the dogs are separated, put them into their respective safe spaces and ignore them. The length of time you give them the "silent treatment" should vary depending on the seriousness of the fight and the role that each dog played. Some dogs will mellow after about an hour while others cannot be let out until the next day. Whatever the case, make sure both dogs are calm as you slowly re-expose them to one another.

You Are "Top Dog"

As the human in a multiple-dog household, it's your responsibility to educate your dogs in order to manage them properly. The more clicker-cued behaviors your dogs understand, the more versatility you have in creating a safe environment for them. If you manage their environment well, you can keep aggressive behavior from happening in the first place. If aggressive episodes have already taken place, dissect the problem areas, and develop a plan to manage the dogs better and to teach them the skills they will need to implement your plan. Without careful management, aggression may lead to injury, and you may have to give your dog away or, in the worst case scenario, euthanize him. Your commitment to a training program can help you avoid these unfortunate outcomes.

CHAPTER 6

Treating a Dog That Is Aggressive Toward People

Dogs that are aggressive toward people present the most serious canine behavioral problem. Owning a dog that could potentially harm a person, especially a child, is risky business. Many things are at stake. Most important, of course, the possibility that someone could get seriously injured (or worse) must be foremost in your mind; you would feel horrible if your dog were to hurt someone. The repercussions of such a disaster would be far reaching, affecting not only the victim, but potentially you, your family, and your livelihood.

A dog that is aggressive toward humans has a disease, a disease as chronic as diabetes or high blood pressure. Though we can lessen the symptoms considerably via treatment, the sickness itself is never totally cured. The goal is not to cure but to put preventive measures in place to minimize the risk that the dog will ever bite someone again. The treatment includes meticulous management and specific clicker training exercises.

If your dog has been aggressive toward people, you will need to think about what steps to take. The decision of whether or not to attempt to rehabilitate your aggressive dog is a personal one based on many factors: cause, severity of injury, size of the dog, the dog's previous reinforcement history, what the dog's triggers are, family compliance, financial commitment, time commitment, and so on. The list of questions that follow will help with your decision-making process. It is best to consult with a qualified trainer or behaviorist in your area to review the options.

Cause: Why is the dog being aggressive? Did someone abuse the dog before you adopted him? Do children taunt and tease him while you are at work? Or has the dog been showing aggressive signs since he was a puppy? Have you been aware of this behavior? Have you been inadvertently reinforcing it? Certainly we all have a soft spot in our hearts for the dog that has been abused by human hands as compared to the dog that has been exhibiting aggressive behavior since he was a puppy.

Severity of injury: Did the bite require cosmetic surgery? Stitches? Did the dog snap but not actually bite? Growl but not actually snap? The more serious the bite, the greater the chance that this dog might be unable to live with humans safely.

How big is the dog?: Is this an aggressive toy poodle or an aggressive Great Dane? Smaller dogs, for the most part, do far less damage than larger dogs.

Reinforcement history: Has the dog been behaving this way for five years or for five days? How has the family reacted when aggressive behaviors are displayed? How many times has the dog been aggressive? No matter how long the dog has been exhibiting aggressive tendencies, behavior can always be shaped in one direction or another. The brain is fluid. New neural pathways are constantly being built. The question is, how much improvement can be made? And will the behavior improve enough to ensure that the dog's human family members can live with the dog safely?

The triggers: Does the aggression happen only at a certain time of day? Only when Uncle Charlie visits? Or does it happen when anyone visits at any time of day? Is your dog aggressive only when he is eating a stuffed Kong in his crate or is he aggressive when anyone walks by his crate? It is much easier to work with a dog that has fewer triggers than one that is in constant turmoil.

Family compliance: Are the members of your family willing to change their behavior toward the dog? Will they clicker train the dog? Will they follow directions? Will they stop interacting with the dog in the way that they enjoy, for the benefit of the dog? All family members must support each other and work together to help improve the dog's behavior.

Time and money: Do you have the time to devote to managing and clicker training your dog? Do you have the money to employ the help of a trainer or behaviorist? Can you continue the training for at least six months? Consistency is key. You need to have the resources to be able to work with a professional, for at least a couple of months, to see a true change in your dog's behavior. Though clicker training can give you instant results, the behavior has to be repeated enough to develop into a habit. It takes at least six weeks of practice for behavior to become habitual. And even then the temperamental tendency of the dog might be to continue reacting.

As you can see, the list of questions is extensive. Each situation is different. Each dog is different. Each owner has a different set of expectations.

The treatment plans offered in the following pages will decrease the symptoms of your dog's aggression problem, in some cases making them totally invisible to the casual observer. This can, however, be dangerous in itself if you are persuaded into thinking that your dog no longer has a problem. The problem will always be there; it is a question of you and your dog working together to manage the problem behavior.

Through these exercises, the relationship between owner and dog is deepened. The owner is now the leader and the dog is a working, cooperative participant. To be successful, the dog needs his human family members to guide him and tell him which behavior is acceptable and which behavior is not. He now makes decisions in union with the people he lives with, not against them. He is no longer controlling the environment with his undesirable behavior but rather he learns to comfortably control himself amid the most difficult of distractions. If you take away that structure too soon, he will most likely fall back into his old behavior patterns.

For example, recently I worked with a dog that was aggressive to other dogs, joggers, and to anything that "rolled," such as carriages or skateboards. Within a couple of weeks, this dog could walk through any environment, faced with all of the above. Instead of being aggressive, the dog would see the object and look right at her mistress for further instruction. This owner, who formerly could not even walk her dog down the street, could now stroll through neighborhood parks at the busiest time of day. Left on her own, would this dog still chase joggers or threaten other dogs? Probably. However, with the guidance that the owner now provides, this dog will never have to take the initiative to be aggressive again. And over time, the dog's attitude will change from one of reactivity to one of relaxation when confronted with the previously troublesome triggers.

Why is your dog aggressive to *x*? You might know. You might not. It may have been that he was beaten by his former owner, a man, and that's why he gets along so much better with women, or it could be that all of a sudden your dog is now aggressive to children for no apparent reason. It is helpful to be able to understand why a behavior happens, what the dog's motivation for performing it is, but it is not impossible to work with your dog if you do not know the reasons for his bad behavior.

I think of canine behavior as being either desirable or undesirable. Aggressive behavior is not necessarily "good" or "bad"; aggression is, after all, a normal trait in any species. It is, however, indisputably undesirable when a dog exhibits aggression in a human household.

Whatever the level of your dog's aggression problem, you should implement the Core Management Plan presented in this chapter. Then identify your dog's specific undesirable behavior, review the Clicker Training Recipes later in the chapter, and find the training recipe that addresses your dog's particular problem. Read the treatment plan thoroughly and then begin to practice. It is always wise to work with a positive trainer/behaviorist in your area.

If you are unable to dedicate the time and resources that it takes to rehabilitate your dog, depending on the severity of the problem, you must consider finding another home for the dog or, with the help of your veterinarian and veterinary behaviorist, euthanizing the dog. Never relinquish this dog to either a rescue organization or a local shelter without fully disclosing the behavioral history of the dog. As much as you want to save your dog's life, you must allow the organization to make a fair assessment of your dog's behavior for future placement prospects.

Core Management Plan for the Dog That Is Aggressive Toward People

1. Incorporate clicker training sessions into your schedule.

Clicker training challenges your dog's mind as well as teaching him the skills to manage encounters without aggression.

Whether you have a fearful or dominant dog, clicker training is a way to launch a whole new relationship with your dog. Fearful dogs love the confidence that the clicker instills. Dominant dogs are satisfied by the newfound ability to control events in their lives (i.e., the power to make you click).

For both kinds of dogs, frequent clicker sessions—five to fifteen minutes at least twice a day—will not only build new behaviors but will also mentally stimulate them and begin to change their outlook on life.

2. Feed your dog by hand.

If your dog bites you, he must lose the privilege of leisurely eating his meal out of a bowl. From that point forward, he must work for his meal—all of his meal. Feed him by hand or by throwing bits of food near him only when desirable behavior has earned reinforcement. Set up numerous clicker training sessions every day to work on foundation behaviors (see page 38). You can also teach your dog how to experiment with his behavior to earn rewards (see page 65, Creativity). Your dog can begin to eat out of his bowl again only after being "bite-free" for six months. If the dog's behavior worsens, the bowl privilege is removed again.

This aspect of treatment is extremely important because your dog has to understand that he depends on you, and his human family members, for the materials that he needs to survive, mainly the food he eats. Whether or not he will eat is determined by the behavior that he exhibits to his human counterparts. Essential rewards, such as his meals, are no longer handed out freely. He has to work for them.

3. Your dog works for all rewards.

Think of what your dog needs to survive: food, water, the opportunity to urinate and defecate, and so on. These are all necessary and reinforcing—and they are no longer going to be given to the dog unless he earns them. The dog needs to do something positive for you before receiving anything, even praise or petting. For example, if the dog wants to be let out to eliminate, he must sit before you open the door. Click as he sits. The sit (and the click it earns) makes the door open.

If you ask your dog to perform a behavior and he doesn't, simply walk away and ignore him. If he's on lead, escort him into his crate. Leave him there for a bit. Or go into another room and close the door. Wait a couple of minutes and then return. Ask your dog to perform the behavior again. Click and feed any behavior that is a step in the right direction toward the behavior—even if it is merely eye contact. Shape the necessary steps needed to acquire your finished behavior.

This concept is also important because, maybe for the first time in your dog's life, he realizes that he is dependent on you; it's through you that he earns the things in his life that he cherishes. He no longer takes you and his resources for granted. He understands structure and leadership and his role in this equation.

4. **Ignore attention-seeking behavior.**

Your dog practices certain repetitive behaviors that are guaranteed to get your attention: barking, whining, pawing, growling, biting, etc. Identify what those behaviors are and be sure that you never reinforce them. Ignore them. Do not even look at behavior that you do not want to see repeated. To ignore the dog is to totally take your attention away from him: no speaking to him, no motioning in his direction, and no eye contact. We do not want to engage the dog in any way if this is a behavior that we want to be rid of. From this time forward, the only way your dog will earn your attention is to perform an appropriate behavior that you have cued him to do. If your dog has been practicing this unwieldy behavior for a long period of time, you may have to wait an even longer period of time before it disappears entirely. It may, in fact, get worse before it gets better. Your dog might become extremely frustrated when you do not respond to his relentless tantrum. This frustration can increase the risk of a bite. Be careful of getting caught in this cycle. Click and feed only behavior that is calm and cooperative.

5. **Praise and pet for short periods only.**

Praise and pet your dog for a short period of time only after he has earned it. Ask for a sit, click, and then pet and praise your dog for five to ten seconds. Then get up and walk away. Many owners do not think of petting and praise as a reward in itself. It becomes so second nature to us, half the time we do not even realize that we are petting our dog. Teach your dog that petting and praise is something valuable for which he must work.

This is important because, again, we want you to be the one who holds the key to the doling out or withdrawing of your attention. We don't want your dog to have the time to decide he's had enough of your affection; this might lead him to growl at you, which will cause you to definitely want to withdraw your affection. We do not want the dog rehearsing the behavior of: "I growl and humans go away."

6. Do not approach your dog in a threatening way.

Be aware of what your body language is saying to your dog. Common examples of human body language that distress our dogs and can result in a bite include an out-stretched hand, leaning forward over the dog, stepping over the dog, and/or patting the dog on the head. Avoid intimidating your dog simply by the way you move.

7. No roughhousing or tug games!

Allowing your aggressive dog to play rough with anyone, including yourself, sets him up for failure. Dogs that are reactive toward people in general need to learn to respect humans and to practice self-control around humans at all times. If your dog has bitten, he should not be allowed to engage in rough play with you or anyone else. Rough play allows your dog to practice pushing and pulling human clothing and skin, a pastime we do not want the dog to rehearse. Rough play can also overstimulate the dog in a matter of seconds. It can be difficult to regain control of a situation once a dog has started biting.

Instead of rough play, your dog's recreational time should be spent in constructive activities including free shaping, object exchanges, retrieving tennis balls or Frisbees, and other physically and mentally stimulating training exercises.

8.   Keep a long line attached to your dog's collar.

Attach a long line to your dog's collar for added safety. If for some reason you need to escort your dog from one place to another, instead of grabbing the dog's collar, lead the dog by the line instead. In this way, if there is an emergency, you can physically hold the dog away from your body, or a family member can pull the dog off of you. The humans remain in control of the situation. You can purchase a long line from the makers of the Gentle Leader head collar or you can make one yourself. Purchase a thin, nylon line at the hardware store. On one end, attach a clip to attach to your dog's collar. Leave the other end free to prevent your dog from getting snagged on anything in the house. When you attach the line to your dog's collar, remember to click and treat your dog as you put it on and take it off. If your dog is sensitive to your body language, do not bend over the dog. Instead bend at the knees, keep your body straight, and attach the long line from there.

If your dog starts to chew on the line, coat it with a bitter-tasting substance such as bitter apple or lemon juice.

9.   No dogs on the furniture.

If your dog growls when he is lying on the furniture, then that privilege must be taken away immediately. From this point forward, he is allowed on the furniture only when you ask him to accompany you. And, if at any point he growls, you lead him off of the couch by his long line and put him in his crate. When you are not home, section off the room with baby gates to limit his access.

Teach your dog placement cues as well. Cue your dog to jump up on the couch by patting the cushions. Now throw a treat on the floor as you say the word, "Off." As your dog jumps off of the couch, click and throw him another treat. Escort him into another room and give him something more mentally challenging to do. Practice this behavior sporadically. Be careful not to build a behavior chain of him continually jumping on the furniture so that you can continue to call him off.

10. Your dog does not sleep in bed with you.

If your dog has bitten you, do not allow him to sleep in your bed. Dogs that are allowed to sleep at the end of the bed enjoy a great privilege. Your dog's behavior has to be beyond reproach to earn this privilege. This is because while you are sleeping you have no idea what behavior your dog is displaying. You are in your most defenseless position. What if you turn over in your sleep and kick the dog by mistake?

(If your dog is aggressive only toward visitors, you may allow him to sleep on your bed. Ask him to perform a behavior and then invite him up on the bed. If he gets on by himself, cue him to get off. If he displays aggression toward you at any time, the bed-sharing privilege is lost.)

11. Your dog does not pull you on the leash.

Your dog must walk with you politely; no more dragging you down the block. You need to remain in control of your dog at all times for the safety of others as well as for yourself. If you are going to begin desensitizing your dog to various stimuli, you need to be able to control and manage your dog properly. (See page 43, Heeling on a Loose Leash.)

12. Your dog is not allowed to jump up on people.

Your dog needs to be taught self-control in the presence of people. No more jumping up and knocking them down! Put your dog in a Gentle Leader head collar and click and feed for "Four on the Floor" (see page 53). If you do not have the time to train your dog when visitors come over, keep your dog confined in a safe place so that this problem behavior will not continually be practiced. Work on the behavior when you can, so that eventually when visitors do come over, you can click and feed your dog for acceptable behavior. And remember to not reinforce your dog's frenzied behavior when you come home from work.

13. Your dog should always come when he's called.

The days of ignoring Mom or Dad's requests are over! Your dog needs to come to you every time you call him. If you want to let him run, be sure to keep a long line attached to his collar so that when you call him, he has no choice but to come. As your dog's leader, you must be consistent and follow through on all your requests (see Chapter 1, Clicker Home Management).

If your dog is aggressive to either people or other dogs, please keep your dog on a leash at all times. You cannot allow a reactive dog to run free because the risk is always there that he will bite a person or fight with another dog.

14. Double the amount of exercise your dog gets.

Make sure your dog has adequate physical and mental exercise each day. Instead of leaving your dog home alone all day, see if you can bring him to a doggy day care a couple of times per week. Or have a pet sitter come in and exercise your dog in the middle of the day. Be sure to let all personnel know of your dog's behavior problem.

If your dog is not good with strangers or other dogs, then keep him on-leash at all times and take him with you when you walk or jog. Make sure to choose areas where dogs are required to stay on-leash at all times. You can also play retrieval games with your dog in fenced areas such as tennis courts and baseball fields. Or how about taking private agility lessons? Agility training is a great way to build confidence in the fearful dog. Through agility training, your dog not only learns how to learn, but he can also explore and experiment with different obstacles that he previously might have been afraid of. For example, many dogs with fear issues find standing on skinny surfaces, such as walking on the dog walk and the teeter-totter, to be especially challenging. As the dog successfully faces his fears, his emotional horizons are broadened.

The more you can safely exercise your dog, the less likely your dog might be tempted to engage in aggressive behavior of any kind. A tired dog is a happy dog!

15. Practice safe home management.

If you know your dog is more of a threat at certain times of the day, or if there is a certain set of circumstances that governs whether or not he will bite, please be proactive and put the dog in his safe space with a mentally stimulating toy if these circumstances arise. For example, if you know your dog does not do well with strangers in the house, confine your dog in a safe space at least a half hour prior to the visitors coming. Do not leave it up to fate whether or not your dog will react.

16. Toys are earned and rotated daily.

Rotate your dog's toys each day. Let's say your dog has ten toys. Put all ten in a cabinet or drawer and each day give your dog two or three new toys. Make sure to ask for behavior before the dog is allowed access to his toy. At the end of the day, pick up the toy(s), put them away, and choose a couple more for the next day. (Don't give your dog any chew toys unless he is kept in his safe area. We would not want visitors to be walking by and mistakenly run into the dog who is chewing on his bone.)

It is important to rotate the dog's toys and keep a tight rein on access to them. Toys are highly reinforcing to your dog. Gaining access to them is a privilege that he has to earn.

Training Recipes: Managing Specific Aggressive Behaviors

Now that your Core Management Plan has been put in place, define your dog's specific aggression issue and begin to treat the behavior by following the recipe that corresponds to the behavior. Read through the written description first and then gather any equipment you will need. Please note that as much as I would love to give you a "cookie cutter" recipe to solve your dog's problem, that's just not possible; every dog, and every handler, is different, so there's no such thing as "one size fits all." That is why I always recommend that you work with a qualified professional.

In these recipes, punishment is never used (except for the occasional "time-out"). At no time, during any of the exercises, will you be luring your dog (showing your dog the treat first). Instead you will reward the dog for behavior that has already been performed. This is standard operating procedure for correct clicker training, and one of the greatest benefits of using the clicker as a learning tool: it helps you practice true teaching, rather than just bribery.

Eating in Peace

This exercise will teach your dog to feel comfortable if humans are around him when he's eating.

Especially helpful when…

- You have visitors and they unknowingly walk by the dog while he is eating.
- Your children have friends over and your dog snatches a cookie from one of their hands. In his haste to eat the treat, he drops some onto the floor. One of the children hurriedly starts to gather up the dropped food with her hands.

How to make it happen:

1. Pick up your dog's food bowl; don't leave it on the floor all day. He will now work for his meal each day. The opportunity to eat is to be earned, not assumed.

2. Make sure you have implemented the principles of the Core Management Plan.

3. Attach a long line to your dog's collar.

4. Sit in a chair with your dog's food bowl in your lap.

5. Cue your dog to do simple behaviors like sits, downs, backing up, etc.

6. Click and feed your dog a couple of pieces of kibble for compliant behavior.

7. Click and feed your dog for any behavior that displays self-control around the food bowl.

8. Repeat Steps 4 through 7 several times, until your dog has had his full meal.

9. After your dog gets comfortable with you sitting in a chair, now seat yourself on a lower stool with his food bowl in your lap.

10. Repeat Steps 5 through 7 several times.

11. With success, lower your body closer to the floor.

12. Repeat Steps 5 through 7 several times.

13. Once you are seated on the floor, click and feed your dog for calm behavior.

14. As your dog's behavior continues to improve, put three pieces of kibble in an empty bowl.

15. Put the bowl down on the floor, and stand next to the bowl.

16. Click for calm behavior and allow your dog to eat the pieces of kibble out of the bowl.

17. Repeat Steps 14 through 16, while continuing to stand next to the bowl, until the meal is finished.

18. Slowly increase the amount of kibble in the food bowl.

19. Once your dog is eating kibble out of his food bowl without event, have family members walk by, click, and drop your dog's favorite treats—for example, pieces of turkey, chicken, pepperoni—into his bowl.

20. Have the family members click and treat for each of the following criteria:
    - With each step as they walk toward the dog while he's eating.
    - With each step as they walk by the dog while he's eating.
    - With each step as they walk around the dog while he's eating.
    - As they stand in one spot near where he's eating.
    - As they stand in one spot and talk low near where he's eating.
    - As they stand in one spot and talk louder near where he's eating.
    - As they stand in one spot and move their arms near where he's eating.
    - If the dog looks up while he's eating.
    - If the dog looks up at them while he's eating.

The goal is for humans to be able to move in and around the dog while he is eating.

21. Here are the steps for the end behavior:
    - Make the meal.
    - Ask the dog to perform a behavior like a sit or down.
    - Click and set the dog's meal on the floor.
    - If the dog should show aggressive signs at any point, take your dog's line and heel him away from the bowl. Put your dog in his time-out space for two to three minutes and back up to clicking and feeding the dog for appropriate behavior only.

Secrets of success:

- If your dog guards his food bowl around strangers, then feed your dog only in a private, secure area away from people. You don't want him practicing the guarding behavior.
- If your dog guards his food around other dogs, then feed your dogs separately. (For tips on how to establish a feeding-time routine, see "Name Recognition," page 135, in the chapter on multiple-dog households.)
- If you have more than one dog, feeding them separately is always a good idea. This way, you always know how much each individual dog is eating. You also do not want the dogs stealing food from each other; this is how many dogs become obese.
- If your dog acts aggressively only if someone pets him while he's eating out of his bowl, do not allow him to eat out of the bowl. Instead, pet him once, click, and give him a small handful of food either in your hand or by placing it on the floor in front of him. This is how he will eat his meal.

Aggression prevention tips:

- Hand feed your dog for a limited time.
- Sit with your dog's bowl in your lap, click, and feed him wonderful treats as he is eating his meal.
- Walk by your dog, and as he is eating, click as you drop great treats into his bowl.

Object Exchange

Work on this recipe if your dog is aggressive when he is holding on to a "stolen" item or a favorite toy and a person walks by or tries to take the object.

Especially helpful when…

- Your dog has toys strewn all over the house. You have a surprise visitor. You have no time to pick up the toys before the newcomer walks into the house.
- A family member sees the dog with a cute toy. Playfully, he or she reaches down and tries to wrestle it out of the dog's mouth.
- Your dog steals a candy wrapper. Your friend, fearing for the dog's safety, tries to take the wrapper out of the dog's mouth.

How to make it happen:

1. Give your dog an object that he considers worthless.
2. Tell your dog to "Drop."
3. Click just as your dog releases the object.
4. Feed your dog for compliance. If your dog will not release the item initially, show him the treat first (as a lure), and then as he drops the item to get the treat, say "Drop." Follow up with a click and another treat. As your dog gets more comfortable with this behavior, say "Drop" and take the object before showing him the treat. Then click and treat (reward) him for the relinquishment of the object.
5. Give the item back and repeat Steps 1 to 4.
6. On the last exchange, simply get up and walk away when your dog drops the object. Do not click and feed your dog.
7. Leave the item with your dog. If you'd rather not leave the item with your dog, throw a handful of treats on the floor and, while your dog is eating the treats, pick up the object and put it in a secure area.
8. Work approximately two to four exchanges per session.

9. As your dog becomes more successful with this behavior, over several sessions slowly increase the "value" of the object you are asking him to "Drop." Start with worthless items like chewed-up stuffed toys and move on to higher-valued items such as Kleenex, shoes, and so on.

Teach the object exchange:

1. Give your dog an object that he is not very possessive over.

2. Click and throw treats on the floor as you approach your dog. Always use treats that are of a higher value than the object that the dog has in his mouth. Use a high rate of reinforcement. Approach your dog from the side, not head-on, and click and feed as you move toward him. Let your dog eat freely.

3. Click and throw treats on the floor to reward him for allowing you to watch him interact with the object. Eventually, when your dog hears the click, he will readily drop the object in his mouth to eat the treats. As you continue to work this behavior, put the action of the dog releasing the item on cue:

   • Just before he drops the object, say "Drop."

   • Reinforce with clicks and treats.

   After eating, he may or may not pick up the object again. Do not try to take the object away at this point; rather, pick it up and give it back to him if you can.

4. Repeat Steps 1 through 3 until your dog feels comfortable with you near him while he has the object.

Secrets of success:

• While working on this behavior, keep any other items that the dog would consider valuable off of the floor in the surrounding area.

• Make sure your dog is hungry before starting the session.

• Use soft, highly palatable treats when working on this behavior.

• Make sure your dog values the type of food you are feeding him more than he values the particular item you want him to relinquish.

- Practice object-exchanging sessions several times a day.

- Work four to five days with one object before moving up to the next level (an object that is even more desirable to your dog).

- Success builds upon success. Move to the next level only after your dog has mastered the previous level.

- If your dog shows any signs of aggression, it means you went too far, too fast. Back up to the previous level and work from there.

- Don't take as great a jump with the next object as you had with the previous.

- If there are only a few specific items that your dog constantly guards, then change your dog's associations with those items by teaching your dog to touch, hold, and retrieve these items on cue. (See "Targeting" on page 45 and "Hold an Object" on page 60.) These fun, constructive behaviors will replace the old, possessive behavior.

- Keep a long line on your dog while practicing these exercises. This allows you to keep control of him if he should become aggressive; you can hold him away from your body, stabilize him so that he cannot chase anyone, or simply escort him into his safe area.

- If you do not feel safe approaching your dog while he is in possession of an object, simply walk away and ignore the dog. Your safety is always paramount, regardless of the object your dog has.

Aggression prevention tips:
- Practice object exchanges with your dog from the very beginning.
- Never forcefully pull anything out of your dog's mouth.
- If your dog should steal something, try not to make a big fuss. Simply go to the dog and practice an object exchange.

Please note:

If you have a dog that steals things constantly, make sure to always have a long line on your dog in the house. This way, if your dog should steal something, you can simply pick up the line and walk forward briskly. Heel the dog until he drops the object. Quicken your pace if needed. Walk the dog outside if you need more room. (Many dogs love to lie down and devour items, but once you ask them to perform an incompatible behavior, such as heeling, they readily drop the object.)

Warning:

• Under no circumstances should you ever chase your dog, tackle him, or corner him to pull an object forcefully out of his mouth. This is a sure way to get bitten.

Sharing the Space

If your dog aggressively guards certain locations like his bed, the couch, or his crate, you can teach him to be more generous with "his space" by training him to get on or off the area on cue.

Especially helpful when…

• Your dog growls at you every time you walk by him when he's on his bed.
• Your dog threatens you every time you want to sit in your favorite chair.
• Your dog will not allow you to get into your own bed.

How to make it happen:

1. If you can, take away or deny access to the items that your dog is guarding. Reintroduce them at a later date, if ever.
2. Make sure you have implemented the principles of the Core Management Plan.

3. First teach your dog to jump up on an object, such as the bed or couch, on cue:
   • Pat the object, telling your dog to "Up."
   • When your dog jumps up, click and praise him.

4. Then teach your dog to get off of the chosen object on cue:
   • Ask your dog to "Off" as you either entice him off or guide him off with your long line.
   • Click and give delicious treats as your dog's feet touch the floor. You want the dog to like jumping off of the object more than getting on.

5. Perfect this behavior with a variety of objects, not necessarily just areas of contention. For example, teach your dog to jump up and off of hassocks, grooming tables, gallon drums, and pause tables (be sure he has the agility needed to jump onto the chosen object). Be creative. Feel free to shape the behavior.

Secrets of success:

• While working on this behavior, put away the objects that your dog might guard.
• Put up baby gates so that the dog cannot gain access to the specific problem areas.
• Leave a long line on your dog so that you can follow through if the dog does not comply with your request to get off a certain object or area.

Aggression prevention tips:

• Clicker train your dog to jump on and off objects on cue.
• Teach your dog to say "Please" should he want access to a certain area.
• Change the location of dog beds and crates so that the dog doesn't guard one area or another.

Living Together in Harmony

When your dog is aggressive to you, the owner, it makes for a less than happy home. This six-week program helps make things more secure for both of you.

Especially helpful when…

• You just want to relax and enjoy the relationship you have with your dog.

How to make it happen:

1. Week One

    (a) Feed your dog by hand.

    • Ask your dog to sit.

    • Click and feed a few pieces of kibble.

    • Continue until the meal is finished.

    • Feed your dog twice a day.

    (b) Begin to clicker train your dog.

    • Work on the following Foundation Behaviors: sit, eye contact, stay.

    • Practice two to four times a day; one to three minutes each session to start.

    (c) No roughhousing or tug-of-war games.

    (d) Limit your dog's access to the furniture and bedroom.

    (e) When you are home, attach a long line to your dog's collar if necessary. Remember to click and treat your dog when you put it on and take it off.

    (f) Double the amount of physical exercise your dog gets.

2. Week Two

    (a) Ask your dog to say "Please" before you grant him any of the following requests: eating, petting, praising, opportunity to eliminate, playing, anything else the dog may want.

    (b) Praise and pet your dog for short periods only.

(c) Ignore all attention-seeking behaviors like whining, barking, or pawing. Get up and walk into another room if necessary. Feel free to escort your dog to his time-out space via the long line.

(d) Continue clicker training your dog as in Week One.

3. Week Three

(a) Toys are rotated on a daily basis.

(b) Continue with your clicker training sessions in which you work on the Foundation Behaviors. Add the recall and loose leash heeling exercises (see Chapter 2). Slowly lengthen your sessions.

4. Week Four

(a) Implement the emergency recall cue (see page 62).

(b) Continue your clicker training exercises. Begin working on the Down (see page 41). Also experiment with the free-shaping exercise on page 65.

5. Week Five

(a) Take a clicker training class.

(b) Continue practicing all of the previous steps in this recipe.

6. Week Six

(a) Customize your clicker training program by working on the specific areas where your dog might be the weakest. For example, if your dog guards his toys, review the Object Exchange recipe on page 158.

(b) Continue to implement your Core Management Plan.

Secrets of success:

- Keep a long line on your dog while practicing these exercises. If for some reason your dog should become aggressive, the line will allow you to remain in control of him: you can hold him away from your body, stabilize him so that he cannot chase anyone, or simply escort him into his safe area. Someone else can also use the line to pull the dog off of you, if that should become necessary.

- It is very important that you continue clicker training your dog as well as implementing the Core Home Management Plan on an ongoing basis. Remember, your dog has a disease, the steps outlined here are his treatment. If you stop the treatment, your dog's condition can worsen considerably.

Aggression prevention tips:

- Socialize your dog properly.
- Clicker train your dog.
- Implement some sort of management plan immediately upon the dog's arrival.
- As hard as it is, try not to overindulge your dog's wishes. Aggression can easily become the mark of a "spoiled" dog.
- Do not use punishment-based training techniques on your dog. Aggression can be a side effect, as can other abhorrent behaviors.

Repairing Relationships

Sometimes a dog is aggressive only toward one particular member of the family. If this is the case in your home, this recipe will help.

Especially helpful when…

- You have to go on a trip and the only person at home to take care of the dog is the one that the dog is aggressive toward.

How to make it happen:

1. Have the "targeted" family member follow the six-week program outlined in the "Living Together in Harmony" recipe on pages 163–164.
2. Have the rest of the family members ignore the dog for this limited time. The member of the family that the dog has been aggressive toward has to become the new canine caretaker. All other family members must support him or her in this endeavor.

Secrets of success:

- The "targeted" family member must want to take an active role in this dog's life in a positive fashion. Many times, this family member's feelings are hurt, especially if he or she has been bitten by this dog, and it is hard to forgive and move on.

- All other family members must be supportive and agree to take a "back seat" while this program is being implemented.

- If the dog misbehaves and tries to seek consolation from a favored family member, that individual must not reinforce the dog for seeking solace with someone other than his new guardian.

Aggression prevention tips:

- All family members need to take an active role in the dog's training and socialization.

- Your dog needs familial structure.

- All members of the family should clicker train the dog.

- One member of the family should not overindulge your dog's wishes.

- Do not use punishment-based training techniques on your dog. The important thing is that all family members be consistent with the way they communicate with your dog. Otherwise your dog will be confused and might pick sides.

Greeting Gracefully

If your dog is aggressive to visitors to your home, you must teach him to be more accepting of the new people. But first, you must manage your dog's behavior. Never permit your dog to run to the door in a threatening way. His inhospitable behavior, if you allow it, will continue to occur because by allowing the behavior you are reinforcing it.

Especially helpful when...

- You have many family members and neighbors who visit frequently, sometimes unannounced.
- You would like your dog to be able to welcome guests in a much more controlled manner.

How to make it happen:

Part I: Management

1. All family members must follow the Core Management Plan (see page 146). Your dog needs to know that all humans in the family are his leaders. If he fully understands this, your dog will realize that he does not have the right to decide who can and cannot enter the home. This decision is left up to the humans in the family. Your dog must respect this decision by exhibiting some self-control if cued to do so.

2. If you cannot clicker train your dog upon the visitor's arrival, then crate your dog before they come.

    (a) The crate should be in a place where the dog cannot see the guests. Seeing the guests from his crate could overstimulate your dog and actually exacerbate his aggression problem. If you anticipate that your dog will be noisy, choose the most distant room in the house.

    (b) Ask your visitors to ignore the dog. Make sure no one sneaks away and "visits" your dog.

(c) Put your dog in his crate with a mentally stimulating toy.

(d) Leave the dog there until you are ready to work with him to follow the clicker training steps in Part II.

Part II: Clicker Training

Initially your goal is for your dog to remain calm while your guests are in your home.

1. Prepare for the session.

    (a) Put your dog's head collar on him. Muzzle your dog if you feel it is appropriate to do so.

    (b) Attach a leash to your dog's head collar.

    (c) Get your clicker and some delicious treats.

    (d) Work in several short sessions. One to three minutes per session is plenty to start. As your dog continues to improve, work in three- to five-minute increments.

    (e) Maintain a very high rate of reinforcement throughout the session.

    (f) Be on alert for overstimulation. If your dog becomes overstimulated after five minutes, limit the session to two minutes.

    (g) After the session, put your dog back in his safe space.

2. Begin working with your dog in a room next to where your guests are.

3. Click and feed your dog as you walk around the empty room. Click and feed your dog for each step he takes with you. Click and feed for calm behavior.

4. Every so often, walk into the room where the guests are seated. Ask your visitors to ignore you and your dog.

5. Click and feed your dog for seeing the guests, hearing them, and so on. Let him look at the guests deliberately, then click and feed him for doing so. It doesn't matter what body position he is in. You are clicking for tolerance only.

6. Build up the time that you and your dog are working in the room where your guests are seated. Click and feed your dog for walking with you, sitting quietly by

your side, or lying calmly at your feet.

7. Now you can ask your visitors to help. Click and feed your dog for the following:

   • The visitor looks at the dog for a brief moment and then ignores him. Build up the duration.

   • The visitor talks to the dog briefly and then ignores him. Build up the duration.

   • The visitor moves slightly in some fashion.

   • The visitor makes a bigger move such as getting up from the couch or going to the door.

   • The visitor walks back and forth while your dog is in a sit/stay. The visitor builds up speed.

   • The visitor walks all the way around the dog.

   • The visitor approaches the dog with no eye contact, from the side, while the dog is in a sit/stay or down/stay.

   • The visitor faces the dog frontally then walks away.

   • The visitor faces front and looks at the dog briefly.

8. Gradually increase the time the visitor is with you and the dog. Sometimes the visitor should be looking at the dog, sometimes not. The body positions of you and your visitor should be relaxed and natural. Eventually, the visitor should be able to stand, with you and your dog, in a relaxed manner for a prolonged period of time.

9. If you feel it is safe to do so, ask your visitor to clicker train your dog.

   (a) Give your visitor the clicker and treats.

   (b) Hand your visitor the leash. (Put a second leash on your dog for you to hold, in case of an emergency.)

   (c) Explain to your visitor that no words are necessary. The clicker does all the "talking."

   (d) At first, the visitor should click and feed the dog for simply keeping four feet on the floor. Then the visitor can move on to clicking and treating for each step he or she takes (gently) toward the dog, or for any movement made in the dog's immediate presence.

(e) Tell the visitor beforehand what behavior you will want her to ask for. (Choose a single-cued behavior that your dog already knows. Touching a target stick works beautifully here—see page 45.)

(f) The visitor clicks when your dog performs the desired behavior, then tosses the treats on the floor. The visitor should not reach down or bend over to feed the dog, and he or she should avoid jerky hand movements.

(g) If your dog does not perform the desired behavior, step in and help your dog. (The visitor should never be the one to discipline your dog!) You want your dog to know that this is a united front and that you are backing your visitor. When your dog does accomplish the desired behavior, the visitor will then click and toss the treats on the floor.

10. As your dog becomes more open to working with a handler other than yourself, start to ask other visitors (one at a time) if they would like to clicker train your dog. The more people your dog gets used to working with, the more receptive your dog will be when meeting new people. Strangers have now become the new source of clicker training sessions, a fun and stimulating activity.

The goal is to keep your dog happily working while he is being exposed to the unfamiliar person. The more your dog works with the stranger, the more your dog is being reinforced for positive interaction; therefore, the calmer your dog will be as he is exposed to more and more people.

Secrets of success:

- Double your dog's physical and mental exercise before exposing him to a stranger. Usually a tired dog is not in the mood for a confrontation.
- Make sure the dog is hungry—not famished, but ready to eat. Let these clicker training sessions become your dog's meal. The dog knows his meal is dependent on his appropriate behavior. Food is a powerful motivator!
- When working with your dog, remember you may need to click and feed at the lowest intensity of the desired behavior initially. As you continue to work, your dog will perform the desired behavior in its complete form and the aggressive behavior will be silenced.
- Make a plan of action with your visitors before the dog actually enters the room.
- Teach the dog a fail-safe recall (see page 49), or make sure your dog has learned the emergency recall cue (see page 62), so you can use either if the situation becomes alarming.
- It might be beneficial to take your dog out first to meet the visitor before he or she actually enters the house. I had one client whose dog had no problem with visitors as long as the dog was taken outside to meet the person before he or she entered the house.
- Teach your dog that the doorbell or a knock on the door is a signal to go to his safe space (see "Kennel Up When Visitors Arrive" on page 55).
- Try changing the point of entry where visitors enter the house.
- Visitors should not roughhouse or play tug games with the dog at any time.
- Never leave your dog alone with the visitors!
- Remember that thresholds and durations vary from dog to dog.
- Always practice successful sessions with your dog.
- Know your dog's individual limitations.

Aggression prevention tips:

- Introduce your dog to many different kinds of people.
- Let your dog go to "puppy sleepovers."
- Clicker train your dog from the very beginning.
- Ask other people to clicker train your dog as well.
- Beware of the following human body language cues that are intimidating to the dog: outstretched hands, direct eye contact, leaning toward the dog, bending over the dog, stepping over the dog, and patting the dog on the head, neck, or back. These are the most common human signals that may provoke a dog to bite.
- A wagging tail can be a sign of stress; it is not always a sign of happiness or friendliness.
- Continue socializing your dog well into his middle-age years.

Becoming Child-Friendly

If your dog is aggressive toward any of the children in the family, you will need to think long and hard about what to do. The decision of whether or not to rehabilitate the dog depends on three factors: (1) the degree of aggressiveness of the behaviors (snapping, growling, and/or biting) exhibited, (2) the maturity of the child involved, and (3) the family's commitment to working with the dog to ensure the child's safety.

Some dogs get overly rambunctious with children because a roughhousing and wrestling type of relationship has been encouraged. Depending on the age and maturity of the children, it's possible to recondition a dog that has become accustomed to this type of behavior.

A dog that intentionally stalks the child and bites severely, however, presents an entirely different situation; this dog needs to be removed from the home immediately. Though you may be able to improve the relationship between your dog and your child, your child will always be at risk, no matter how pleasant your dog might seem. Remember, aggression is a normal canine behavior—there is no fail-safe "cure" for it. And once the behavior has been rehearsed, there is a good chance that it will be repeated.

Any dog that has bitten a child severely enough to break the skin should be immediately removed from the household. The risk of the dog biting again is simply too high. This is especially true if the child is a toddler or a child that is unwilling or unable to understand the necessary steps that have to be taken to try and remedy the situation.

If placing the dog in another home is an option, the dog will need a home where he will never be in contact with children. Rarely can this truly be accomplished. And, please note, that if you do give the dog away, you could still be liable if the dog bites someone.

The decision of whether or not to keep your dog should be made with the help of a behavioral expert in your area. Use the techniques in the following training recipe as part of your decision-making process.

Especially helpful when...

• Your family loves the dog but for some reason the dog has snapped at one of your children. The family wants to try and work with the problem before deciding on the next course of action.

How to make it happen:

1. The family should immediately implement the Core Management Plan presented earlier in this chapter (see page 146).

2. The child is never, ever left alone with the dog. The dog remains in his safe space until the adults in the family come home.

3. Keep a long line attached to the dog's leach when the dog is in the house and people are home, in case of an emergency.

4. The child is never allowed to roughhouse or play tug-of-war with the dog.

   (a) The only interaction your child will have with the dog is to clicker train him. An adult always supervises the training sessions.

   (b) Clicker training sessions are short, three to five minutes is plenty.

   (c) Lengthen the sessions as the dog's behavior improves and the child's confidence grows.

   (d) Watch for overstimulation. At the first signs, end the session and work for a shorter period next time.

5. Clicker Training Program:

   (a) Work on Foundation Behaviors (see Chapter 2). The child, if mature enough to take part in a training exercise (probably no younger than eight, and always with an adult supervising) should hold the clicker. (with an adult always supervising).

(b) Work on shaping exercises (see page 65). Experiment with behaviors that will interest your child, such as teaching your dog to walk on a balance beam, stand on a skateboard, or negotiate an agility tunnel.

(c) Work on specific desensitization exercises targeting the problem behavior, e.g., collar shyness, food guarding, etc. (See related sections in earlier chapters that apply to the behavior in question.)

Secrets of success:

- The child needs to be mature enough to follow the program in this training recipe and the family must be committed enough to see it through.
- All family members (including the child) must be compliant; otherwise the dog needs to leave the household.
- Children are only allowed to interact with the dog in a calm and gentle manner.
- Supervise or separate always!

Aggression prevention tips:

- When adopting a dog, make sure you know the dog's previous reinforcement history if you have children under ten years of age.
- Socializing your dog with lots of children is key.
- Have each of the children clicker train the dog; they should work with standard obedience cues.
- Never allow the children to do annoying things to the dog like poking at his eyes, pulling his tail, or sitting on top of him, no matter how well the dog might seem to tolerate it.
- Teach your children to respect the dog's space.

A Final Word

Canine aggression can be a very frightening and difficult behavior to work with. Though the rehabilitation process is ongoing, instituting the following two principles can help make tremendous strides toward healing the aggressive behavior: (1) meticulous management so that the dog will no longer rehearse the behavior, and (2) an effective clicker training program that will help reshape the dog's attitude to what he considers aversive.

The beauty of using the clicker is that it "speaks" the same language to all species. It means the same thing, all the time. It is a direct line of communication between teacher and learner.

The importance of the click is the information that it conveys. Behavior is either "desired" or "undesired." There are no confusing gray areas. The dog being trained via the clicker is empowered by the information he accumulates in the process. The same is true for all living creatures: the more information we have, the more we understand about our environment, the more confident we feel, and the better decisions we will make. Now, all of a sudden, things make sense. There is a rhyme to the reason. The world opens up, with its endless array of creative activities, and the behavioral issues that previously were overwhelming now have little significance.

Though aggression cannot be "cured" completely, we can teach our dogs to calmly look at what has frightened them in the past. We can teach them to look at us, as their leaders, and entrust themselves to our care. We can also teach them, via clicker training, a remarkable set of skills that can be used in any situation. These skills can help manage and control aggressive behavior.

Some of the techniques in this book you will be familiar with and some will be totally foreign. Keep your mind open and forever questioning and experimenting.

This book is a work in progress. There is so much more to learn about dogs and our relationships with them, on both scientific and spiritual levels. My goal was to share with you all the information that I have collected through my experiences with Ben and his canine companions, as well as the many unexpected successful solutions imparted to me by my students.

My hope is that you will treat your dog's aggressive behavior as you would any other behavior, without the emotional entanglements that can inhibit your dog's progress. In times of despair and difficulty, please remember: "It's only behavior."

Resources

New Clicker Trainers

Clicking With Your Dog Step-by-Step in Pictures, by Peggy Tillman

Click for Joy, by Melissa Alexander

Getting Started: Clicker Training for Dogs, by Karen Pryor

Learning Theory

Don't Shoot the Dog, by Karen Pryor

Applied Behavior Analysis, by Paul Chance

Behavior Modification, by Garry Martin and Joseph Pear

Behavior Principles in Everyday Life, by John and Janice Baldwin

General Positive Learning

The Culture Clash, by Jean Donaldson

The Power of Positive Training, by Pat Miller

How Dogs Learn, by Mary Burch

Behavior Texts

Applied Dog Behavior and Training, Volume One, by Steven Lindsay

Applied Dog Behavior and Training, Volume Two, by Steven Lindsay

Clinical Behavioral Medicine for Small Animals, by Karen Overall

Canine Body Language

Canine Language, by Roger Abrantes

Calming Signals, by Turid Rugaas

Canine Aggression

The Cautious Canine, by Patricia McConnell

Leader of the Pack, by Patricia McConnell

Feeling Outnumbered, by Patricia McConnell and Karen London

The Canine Aggression Workbook, by James O'Heare

Aggression in Dogs, by Brenda Aloff

Clickers and Clicker Training Gear

www.clickertraining.com
KPCT Waltham, MA 02453
1-800-47CLICK (toll-free in the US)
or 781-398-0754

Head Halters

Dog Training With a Head Halter, by Miriam Fields-Babineau

Raw Diet

Give Your Dog A Bone, by Ian Billinghurst

Natural Health for Dogs and Cats, by Richard Pitcairn and Susan Pitcairn

Holistic Guide for a Healthy Dog, by Wendy Volhard and Kerry Brown

Recommended Websites

www.clickertraining.com (clickers and clicker training info)

www.dogwise.com (books)

www.sitstay.com (head halters)

www.Kong.com (Kong toys)

www.tteam-ttouch.com (Tellington Touch)

About the Author

Emma Parsons, APDT, NADOI, is the Canine Behavior Training Consultant for the VCA Rotherwood Animal Hospital in Shrewsbury, Massachusetts, as well as the Training Director for Karen Pryor's Clicker Training. Her training service, The Creative Canine, specializes in managing and reducing canine aggression and teaching pet owners how to successfully integrate secondhand dogs into new households. Emma is a faculty member of ClickerExpo, and has taught clicker training classes in conjunction with Tufts Veterinary School of Medicine and Yankee Golden Retriever Rescue. She is a member of the National Association of Dog Obedience Instructors, the Association of Pet Dog Trainers, the Heritage Trail Keeshond Club, the New

England Dog Training Club, Massachusetts Animal Coalition, and the Massachusetts Federation of Dog Clubs and Responsible Dog Owners. Emma holds a B.A. from the University of Lowell and looks forward to pursuing her Master's Degree.